ISBN: 9781723788413

M.Stow12

Odin

Freya

Sedna and Ororo Mohawk

EarthCentre: The End of the Universe:

New edition with Creative Commons photo-illustration plot summary references and text notes critically updated.

EarthCentre: The End of the Universe. An Epic Drama.

An Existential-Anthropic Odyssey

An eschatological mystery re-solved

'the frontiers of the spirit'

Part One. An epic funfairgroundride through the EarthCentre theme park of the past present and future...world mythology and religion, cosmology and The Earth and human sciences a graphic novel proem: we create ourselves...

Love and the gentle heart are one thing

as the wise man puts it in his verse

and each without the other would be dust

as a rational soul would be without its reason.

Dante: La Vita Nuova verse 20

My stuttering verse with its uncertain notes
A shudder takes me: tear on tear entire
The firm heart feels weakened and remote:
What I possess seems far away from me
And what is gone becomes reality.

Goethe: Dedication from Faust.

EarthCentre: The End of the Universe: *An Anthropic Odyssey: Being a topological themed mystery ride through: The Cosmos; with dialogue and commentary to be spoken or read in parts at a smooth and rapid-pace and then again slower as an echo in memory and in voices and verses selected by the reader/speaker...*

Part One: EarthCentre.

1.1. Departure (the LifeShip leaves Earth)

-EarthCentres!

-Welcome to: The End of the Universe...
Irreversible temporal-turning terse determining-mentors'
Tilting toppling wobbling tipped averse purposeful contemplators'
Misty-gladed grazed glazed once glacial gazed-over.

Annual-seasonal circumpolar sloped terr-aqueous medium-sized planet.
Volcanic-vapourous pouting spouting coiling broiling boiling-eruption
Crenellate causeway sweeping steeped peaked and troughed.
Surging crashing salt-rock seas coughed and spluttered
Muttering-material vitality now kilometres-high
Super-heated the stewing spewing skies
Stage-plates loosed no sooner risen
As loco-moting steeples' stalking walking upright talking
Swooping trooping cloud-plateau whooping
Terraced-topped raised Terrible-Trees...*
Up-rooted as up-sprung as Autumnal-leaving.

As Each of Us: now as over a blind-wall glooming zooming

Pluming-quailing quagmire sludging

In-exorably craving inter-tidal a-rounding out...

Pitched switching patched *stinging stringing a st*riding-out
Way-sailing singular photo-tropic Solar-burst! Now!
Each of Us!* Toward the fixed-facing Lunar leering
Leaning-over as coming in to land.

The *illuminating* scribe as sidereal as quarter-sized as once quarter distanced from
The Sun *dazzling*-irresistible with a hidden dark light *heat*-force *blistering*
In-*flaming re*-enflaming couched louche slouched-unveiling

Shadowy-*grey* cygnet-supplicant occultation.

Transiting swanning grown-lovely as lovingly verifying seductively inclined

Masked-mounted *haunted-nightly starlight-dusting...*

Peninsular-pouring pouched packaged pocketed.

Charmingly alarmingly meant blent metring

 Dis-armingly into so-many outward-bound

Now opposital polar-outpourings

Of some sadness and regretful whim

Only now consequential once wisdoms' warnings

As at the equatorial in the swim

Gravitational-nucleating variant electro-magnetic rounding-out integument.

Pounding larger and smaller swarming-polarities...

Atomic-asteroidal roughened mineral rocky

Metallic-edges. Plastic dis-embodying

Tectonic platelets spelled-out:

>   -Austral-Asian panning-gyre vast novel forests...

>   -Nautilus Whole-Earthed Atlantic promontory...

>   -Whole-Oceanic...

>   -Specific-Pacific...

>   -Original broad-faced lands hot-dusted...

Amazing! Each of Us: As Now! Cast-outward glanced-off:

>   -Antarctic as Arctic...

crumbling-inundation torn drawn-off and away dirty great -*grey* **sooty**
Precipitate particulate now more probable than not.

Once again:

>   -Great Lunar Impact*!

Each particular Universal part.

Re-volving re-solving re-volting

Ab-solving...as headed-away from

Prophetic-Messianic Apocalyptic devastatingly desolate now barren-warren

a-frighted freighted caged rabbits'* rushed.

In sunlit-fielded cavern-caught.

Flushed-out as outward blushed ruddy-veined glass-eyed

Horned-Bull and She-Bear looked-on.

Hunting punted shunted turning following foolishly industrial-*frigid* Space

Dis-porting Draconical adjutant validate

As baked-through Hadean infernal internal-torched.

Super-Solar scorched gloating bloating boating

Gloaming gloomy gleaning gleaming

Stranded stricken nail-bite shielding un-welded a heaving-to

Un-wieldy show-boating haltingly pinafore nightmare floated shore.

Each Our Own planetary-arc panning-across

Smudging sludging as be-grudging

Eccentric tidal-locking outrigger hooked stabilising angular-axis limiting-lilt...

Lonesome now loathsome-librate crushing slushing brooked.

Held trigger sniggering calendrical subduing extremes

Now runaway re-convergent clashed.

Re-colliding crashed confrontational greedily lustfully landed-below

Impounding as once before complex co-lateral compounding-interest

Simply-loaned out careening-cinematic screening-scree.

Together soaring-views

As We as in awe as in a wave *delighting*...

As with another sudden Sun-baked blistering Roar!

Rivering riven granite-*grey* gritstone-gravel

Risen remaining beached breached

Streaming steaming screaming streaked.

Dirt-brown seas leaked seized bleached

A burning-through strato-spherical Ozone-holed. With escape-velocity reached

Orbital-satellite fleet imaging shutter re-ceding re-recording...

Sepia-scenic photo-opportunistic sunblind-slatted

Feigning faintly *fading ceding* slated slotted.

Window-seated d*isquieting* picture-postcard
Holo-grammatic melodramatic briefly glimpsed beyond
As now below as above and sideways' *emotional* excitement...
Seaboard-City riverboard harbouring-Town seen through

Slurrying industrial-yard and housing-estate
De-berthed thundering thudded anvil bell-clapper clapped...

Clanging-clanking following-on hot-convection current.

Flanking tapering diffuse-spectra stacking firestorm-conflagration
River and Ocean-Seaway Road and Railway burned buckled buried and washed-away
Airways dashed to the ground.

Palace-palisade imprisoning-barricade as gritted grain plains-palmed
Over-flying humble-hamlet and village-farm.
Appealing palling pell-mell show-ground funfair

Arcade re-vealed: Theatre Hall and Shopping Mall

Cable-linking office-block Military-school collegiate Hospitaller-Hotel.

Courtyard as possibly well-meaning mainly leaden-laden

Living cloudburst trailing seismic-shockwave culminate.

In-continental judgment circumnavigating
Forbidding foreboding forfeiting fault-lines rifted

Lifted-off dis-charging circum-venting remains
All overgrown and long-since abandoned.

Shifted sifted-out showering in-candescent
Cascade-burst! The Aurora constricting conversant-coalescence.
Overwhelming suffocation-inducing basilar substrate-abduction quake-*shaking*...
The Celestial-Shoreline burgeoning as over-burdening un-burdening re-birthing
Swelling swilling willing obverse-undulate
Inverse-unsuspecting rolling roiling into the once burped abyss*
The *Once*-Planets' skein-thin skin pricked *pierced* as at each window over-viewed.

Overtaking remaining sunken-puddling pooling bubbling a-muddling through.

Paddling peddling* draining *whispering wheezing wispy* demons' dreaming

Screaming whipped-past ice-locked. Fled-by chanced grasping

We as dry-bone thrown-evacuate oceanic-planet.

Snowball melting slaken-out as out of blind rock gazed-back

Apathetic-malevolence gloved silent as silica-staring finger pointed facing-off...*

Withering-slimy grimy rimy-slaking shaking *shimmering* malodorous

A-*glimmering:*

      -F*erro*-fluid...

      - Core-Mag.

      - Micro-bile fuel-cell...

Crusted rusting mantle yellow-*brown* clay-caked dry-air deserted Fireball

The Wasteland.* Ephemeral stellar-baiting in-difference

Outer as inner-fleeting feeling bearing-down gored bloodied-pawed.

Arterial-cut through wounded young-pride

Voiding further-loss spent sold-on as if now *cheaply...*

Our-Own Owned ways made-up as we go...

We Each make Our-Own owned Way *agreeable...*

As what we make of Our-Way

Becomes: The-Way.*

EarthCentre and Moon with solar thermo-nuclear field above and test bomb impact (Pacific) below.

1.2. The-Past Excised.

The Present-taxied extirpating *conditioned-attachment*

Piecemeal taken-up salty and freshly rib-bone caged.

Breasting-bulbous

Each plying playing marrow-bone jelly-ringed rolled

Surviving within each de-spoiled ashen leafy-leaving

Drunken-milky *breathed* in and out...

Seed-brain engaged nerves-ended

In soft-tissue seared sheer bone muscle-fleshed out.

Horripilation a-*shuddering*...

Each of Us: The Universe:

A meteorological journeying

Of mindful-souls*

Atomic-Askance telling pale peeling-back

Drilled- back through-filling

Gnawed-at empathy

Emblematic-seeking.*

Pleading plain-sailing appleine-fallen.

De-seeded chalking-up iso-morphic geo-logic

Halo-genic striate layered meteoric mineral carbon-chondrite

Cordially as ever contrite re-condite cordite rendering-rent.

Belligerent as on blue-green rock-ore re-born

Battered bruised rat-running rutted event
Then rotting-away gnawing as of Graces en-gorged.

As of Furious Fates' be-fallen wraiths' wreathing sciences'-reasoning...

Lunar re-collision departing de-accretion cores.

With each last remaining porous *part*-poured

We! The Living departed.

With Each reluctant yet in-tentional last partly lustily

With no-chance of return as of *nothing* to return-to.

Textural bit-map imaginings tendering self-worth.

Racing ahead remaining remains cordite booming-*resolution*.

Ending-bending re-versal

As returning to The Start starlight *returning*...

Chastening-sped backward to the *very* beginning.

Returning somewhat squeamish squealing screeching Once-

birthed The-Sun's star-rays taken-off.

As not for a first but reverse time rodeo-ring.

Riding waveform coasting conation

Sounding-solation lining-up along the unfixed ferment

Integral par-taking pitted lodestone-loaded.

Damp rank clay-fired freeing preening acerbic vitriolic flexed.

Pliable-plexus Each of Us with throated bloated breath and yells'! As

frozen-out as a-feared flying frying factorial pictorial-resolving.

Anthropo-*scenic now* unitary-primordial muddied-spluttered obscenities

Re-sounding Crying-Out Loud! Each of Us *pixalate* pirating-privateers

Sputtering babbling gurgling gargling delicate-dissipate desiccate estate.

Blasted blown watery-entrapped now

As assuredly only *vaguely* unknowing of The-Way...

Anyway. Pips-squeaked armed and legs flailing wailing as of an All-encompassing

Universal-*onslaught* sped splendid as a cloud-ladder stepped-up...

As over street-scene below.

A worming ribboning

Charming world snake-embracing fine-filtering

Welcoming larder

Warming edible-egg phosphorant electric-eel.

Fondly-differing giggling when it silly-apple

Hated even that then when it juicy-pigeon kept cawing

Clawing rhythmic *funny*-fashion hammering oddly-owling

Singing school-lesson oily pen-happy carrying urging sheep up-the-road.

Within this thin fat-telling very savvy wet yes

Yet visionary voiding blizzard-zoo.

Pouring a goodly grappling-pronouncement

Now! Ice-locked legends keyed-open divergent-diversion...

Vacating-*vacations* held-uniquely redemption seeking a*bsolution*

In *pointful* continuation. *E*xciting exiting ex-acting as ex-tirpating

The devastating-perdition below.

Obliquely as in-stinctively as in-stantly now turning-away...

Each-of-Us: at a time-travelling looking back a re-visiting behind Us.

Each Earthly-*extinction* a better future a future at all only just *hinted*-at...

Inversely. Obversely. Yet, obviously as seen and heard

as felt

Cluttering-*chuttering* crowded-out shielded *shaded-*

out...

glistening pure-Sunlight beaming Heavens' Hellish gleaning.

Felt clattering curving away-from as into an un-Earthly *emptiness*

Back-tracking tessar-act trajectory within The-Radiant.

Reeking over the top-Ness leaking leading then following-on...

Mediating-warmly the intervening vacuity

As early as-*alerted* to:

> -Monstrous!!! The End of Days!

> -The-End of-The-Earth!

> -Life on Earth!

> -*Without* Life...

> - *From:* Earth...

> -With You and Me!

> - Co-Species!

With We apparently the last to leave.

In-ertial as We had come easily to know

Solar-hearted steely muscle-bound nuclear-fielded.

Planetary-cavernous liquid rocky-core and solid-skinned.

The-Once sheltering surrounding rounded-out

Maximal image-filling resolution singly-focused

The once welcoming protecting majestic-magenta...

Lateral vertical projection magnificent mal-efficient *mustering*

Overwhelmingly-*generational* revolutionaries...

Evolutionaries: Those who saw: deep-surface built germinal

Viral dust-cluster cluttering-dermis clad clothed as of an ovule husk and seed-core

Auto-morphic Archean algic-chloroplastid fungal-fern plant stem and shoot.

Conic-culture capturing colonizing phylo-genic proto-zoic up-rooted

Bower-tree flowering towering insect gill-winged pri-mordial fish landed.

Monstrous-walked and crawled and climbed and flew.

Pale-pink flame-lamp zig-zagged ran-raged ragged

As Once to feed perhaps another to seed perhaps another to inculcate.

Perhaps another to incarnate perhaps another to retrieve

As a-*thought* perhaps a memory to spark.

Now! Every known living thing fore-shadowed We! Made Our Mark!

Every plant and mineral and animal-form

That once was and that thus as We survived to tell the story.

Within this intimation of mortality having once been immortal

Forever-Being with those who leave and that which is left behind.

As for a last-time grimaced grinning now as fallen from

As be-fallen from Each Our Own Owned *tiny*-selves passed-across.

Each of Us: snub-nosed snouted luminous now with

The ever-*expanding*...The-Sun. Arrow-headed as metallic flint-stone spearing

energetic filled-*emptiness*... Each of Us: welling in-turn willing *withering* yet writhing
As over a slippery sill-edge went.

As co-ersed erst-while

Not Only by Our Own-Selves but by Each Other. A cursing coursing

Causing reality readily as yet to become en-wombed

Again, as then as to be readily really re-entombed.

Worlds whorled re-roomed cruised-carouselled caroused
Corralled flip-flopped fantastically desperately enchantingly
Dis-enchantingly de-ployed ion-spherical waves-*wavered*...
Won-out...or-else Hope-only dashed. And Faith.
Hope. Pandorian as One
Self-built boat burst of stellar-propellant ploughing
*S*lanted balletic ballistic blasted stifling-rifling
EarthCentre *dawn*...

Drawn aimed and *fired*...spat-out.

A deadly vacuum-avoiding abhorrence

Belly-lashed virescent green hearts-sank

Beyond the habitable comfort-zone leaving...

Error-erasing driven-out.

Driving diving-trajectory de-centring controlling-contrivance

Apparent semblance within applying accepted

Each momentarily pivotal vehement reversal

De-engineering steadily readily as We Go...

Each of Us: attracting as de-tracting

Only ever moving proportional *almost* equal and opposite-forces....

Un-balancing Self-*emptying* as with a reverence

Superficial Outer-reference

Re-filling re-gulating

The Sun-*light* lifted-back towards:

        - Absolute-Zero and the Universal Speed of

Light...

        -Globular-nucleate *e*lectron-magnetite...

        -Gyroscopic-gravitational-gyre...

        -Gimbal gambrel gambol gambling...

        -Jingle-jangling...

Empty-centres... re-treating...

Only *slightly* felt seen and heard.

Of All colour-triad tried reduced mixed-trialed trailed...

As though intrepid of the-*immediate* moment: Real and True.

Nothing-else excepting accepting self-*seemingly* self-controlling

Constant-contesting vitiate variable as within the obviously wittingly possible

Willingly the more probable yet as with inescapable-sleep

Even as in a mechanical dream of the *apparently* impossible.

Remembrance.* A trepidation within taking-over

Personality sex-and-gender wall social-characteristic.

En-crypted im-printed en-coded de-coding *constantly* or not at all...

Long-fused easily occupied oily-plastic metalloid-mineral assemblage

Self-supporting purporting: This *Sporting*-Life* *lit let* split...

Split spilt-out Universal mono-chrome lunar-subtractive...

Heat-fused radio-magnetars split between *pure* **black**-and-white all impure *grey*.

Occlusive recursive insulating-insinuating residue racing...

Measuring-moments: Each-of-Us! Self-*seemingly* perpetual exo-Planetary part.

Minutely-minutia eclipsing Each of Us: living planetary-part.

Now glancing-back as ahead

Of all-shades of an intermittent yellowing-white glow-glared blue-to-red

Red-to-blue...scattering effect *reflective*-inside as outside

V*irtually* un-virtuously

As seen now without-virtue even innocence and/or guilt

Out there without good or evil or love or hatred taken-in.

But a brutal-beauty and terrible-truth.

From the then by-gone

Glowering-grenadine s*yrupy*-Sun

Colliding im-pacting impassioning electric-blue green

From a cyan superfluous now

Universal Deep-Dark Sky. Firstly and seemingly *lastly*

every moment: Shouting! Yelling and cursing

Astronomical rigged-out Robo-nautical

As Beasts of the Field attempting *empty* bellowing in-*anguish*...

As to abattoirial *slaughter* tongue-tied curling-concentrate

Shocked-into-silent dis-belief.

Un-belying bilious-feeling of-Being

Without any immediate or ever any requital.

De-postulating as de-articulating *spooky-token*

spoken: -The Universal Skull!*

From All points Now cosmologically-principled*

All-consuming Universal-Space beyond:

       -Atomic Solar-Orbital...

       -The Galactic-Realm...

       -The Universe!

       - Ourselves!

-Again! Born-Again!!

Co-cavernous *sub*-Solar Polar-Galactic.

Eyeball-socketed rocketed cloudy-flared excited-jawbone and earbone-fared

Variously sidereal-extended as spin-polar pointed-out...

In-consistency *constantly persisting*

Persistently throughout:

     -Special!

     -Theatric!

     -Ourselves!

     -Of Course! As We Are Here! Now!

     -And How? Greater than The-Sum of parts...

     -A-*Port!*

     - A...*Part(s)*...

No upward or downward any longer

No longer inward nor outward bound anymore.

All around Us sidewards faster and faster originating silver-sail.

Gold-plated *wafer*-thin membrane of time and space

Multi-verse strung-alongside de- cycling unfolding until:

     -True! Now!

     -Then?

     -Not Now!

     -Then? Not?

     -Then?

Each Of Our Own Over-lapping unique-key complexion-blent.

Each root and branch-bent catapulted

As variously-askew:

     -Solar-Expanding...

     -The Inflating-Universe...

As of It-Self as of Our-Selves
Solar-chased and chasing away.[*]

Affecting-effective sprung back-plotting procedural bureaucratic-language[*] vent

As yet proto-social Predator-and-Prey storied

Subjected power-relationship parental as pro-scribed pre-scribed...

As continuously re-written non-self selected-out.

As in the aforethought out afterwards *thought-out* blipping-*blazening*

As explained differently exploring retrospective journeys' haptic-historical

Yet hysterical re-conciled with experience...

Ex-foliating expiating as ever one step behind *ahead* beyond

rational-Self... Empirically-headed re-r*easoned*-out reality-

spent

That *is* reality and truly everything *we*-know:

        -Here and Now?

        -Then?

As only ever *almost* and never *exactly* equal or as im-perfectly The-Same.

Exaggerated practically ever more pragmatically identical but then to be differently-

repeated:

        -Here and Now?

        -Then?

As if imaginatively innovating truly-*felt* then as *some* Way meant.

Chosen yet ever f*alsely*-remembered *innocence* hoaxing featherless chicken*

Without Divine Fore-*knowledge** learned told

Observing Observer-*uncertainty**

With Absolute-*necessity* assumed

Self-serving steps necessary decision-making.

Self-firstly the Other beneficial non-absolute *moral*-duty rated raged

Abating bad-will no-one wants caged

In case deluded de-nuded re-turned.

Self- Interest clinched cinched goodly-*excusing*...afterwards preserving

Conditional-hypothetical algorithm: *if/then...what-if ...as if...Or*

Of *that* Other to protect. To-*extract* emotional cognitive sentimental

visceral-*virtue* desirous-wanting as not-wanting something

advantageous *to* ultimate dis-advantage. Failing. The vice of iniquity.

Consequentially. As anything else as not at *this* moment as

Of...that moment...The-Game

Of *fear* not knowing All outcomes:

The unknown always...everbrings: Anxiety.

Anger. Rage. Revenge

Malicious vindictive

Existential-threat...

The Galactic Universal-Skull: two Magellanic nearest local hydrogen-cloud galaxies (eyes) with The–Galaxy as a toothed-grin as if a cosmic wind blowing towards or drawing-in Earth. As seen only from the Southern hemisphere night-sky, through The Galactic Orion spiral arm. Australia.

That moment as all: as willing *some*-assertion never-ending *problematic*

As only *possibility* probability re-solving:

      -The Natural Observable:

      -Universal-Law *observed...*

All-led as by all-else:

      -Universal Golden Silver-Suns' and Golden Galaxies...:*

Kept in good-Grace faint-Hope faithfully *furiously*-Fated

Through every and any opposing hurt and hunger sated.*

1.3. Life-ship: Starship.

So Each Our Own EarthCentre

Each of Us animate intimate Solar-Galactic.

Atomic Time-Zones spanning almost *vacuum*-Space.

Spinnings' spun-out between and within

Wherever We may be and of All-Else

Wherever we may *wish* to be and Never Again

The Present then known as The-Passing.

As at any once staged caged

Prescient potential-accretion cogged clogged wheeling balling

Dodging gambling-shambling rambling:

      -Optimal Warp-Drive...

      -Neutral to negative dropped positively switching forward re-versal...

Attraction-repulsion taken place changing laws as we go...

Revulsion thrown-around and away

Extensively into The-Future as from-The-Past:

      -Nucleic Quark-Neutron to Proton-positronic engineering...

      - Re-programming...

      -Location?

      -Uncertain...

      -Volition?

      -Yes.

Vertigo variable-velocity and *uniquely*-positioned to staying-alive

Utilitarian-*phenomena* pheromonal seeming reflective

Familiarity *making*-sense of or not antagonistic to the *fearful inquisitive*

Only *meaning* to go on more or less...

Relaying relying-upon recurrent-problematic

Imparting categorically re-ducting re-dacting and materially re-solving

Solely and together surviving so Far...so Good.

Uniquely Each-Our-Own Owned Selfie-Selfers to Each-Other and All-Else.

Contrivance-connivance embodying yet eyes wide-open:

      -The Universal Galactic...

      -EarthCentre...

Akimbo-recalled s*miling*-too.

Trapped-outside *strapped-inside*

Stranded with that which is gone

And that which is left behind.

An *almost*-nothingness energetic re-maining

Rested and fed as kitted and fitted-out for survival.

Marooned now as every moment re-installed moved forward

As Each to Each and Each Our Own *vast*-cavern be-calming en-tranced*

Opened to The *fiery*-Sun's st*arry* Shadowy-Lands beyond:

      -Light-Ships!

      -Life-Ship... -

      - Starships!

      -To The LightHouse! Home! EarthCentre! No More!!!

      -No going back now...

      -EarthCentres!

Seen-streaming now un-*flickering lights*

Each unclear un-clouded clearing

Storming rock-islanded *a-w*andering moment.

Bathing amongst yet patently impatiently propelled

As through re-attempting heuristic hu-bristic het-erotic heretic

Combinatorial consequential-choices made.

Whilst ubiquitously turning corners

Attracting and distracting momentarily-momentously continually

Colluding gently phonic-*crackling* amplifying-acquisition...

Wirelessly-widely nervously all-around and across diminishing photonic radiation.

Re-directing directed laser light-waves as if remotely controlling

Self and Other together-controlling switching after-effects...affecting:

Yelling! physical contour-*nestling* tunnelling-and-funneling

Amber-gris vehemently violently violet laser-lit.

The Solar-squall to a *whisper*-quelled.

Welling co-causing All Else to be held in growing-*Trust*

With a caution thrown blown to The Solar-Wind

A glancing blow de-forming formidable starry Nautilus-night.

On All Sides...deadly-*light* daytime

All-potential shades of every *wave-length* frequency and dimension

Vision-able darkness filling-in *invisible a-* passing-through...

Pushed as pulled rare-dust and gas as a dark-water *exposition*

Found merely meme-machine meanly-driven driving scenic-routed

Calculating a-topical as of self-serving and mutual *felt*-synthetic endless-analytic

Inner-mostly learned principled-detachment

Instant-intuition integral personal *dignity*...

Live-feed video wall-monitor's informational diagrammatic*:
Yinlong: Chinese flying flood dragon (springtime) or Azure Dragon of the East.

Below: pulling the carriage of the intertwined creation lovers Nuwa and Fuxi.
as The Galaxy Question-Mark. Greek Scorpion constellation killer of boastful
hunter Orion (or as Babylonian Methusulah: death bringing biblical judgement at
the end of days.

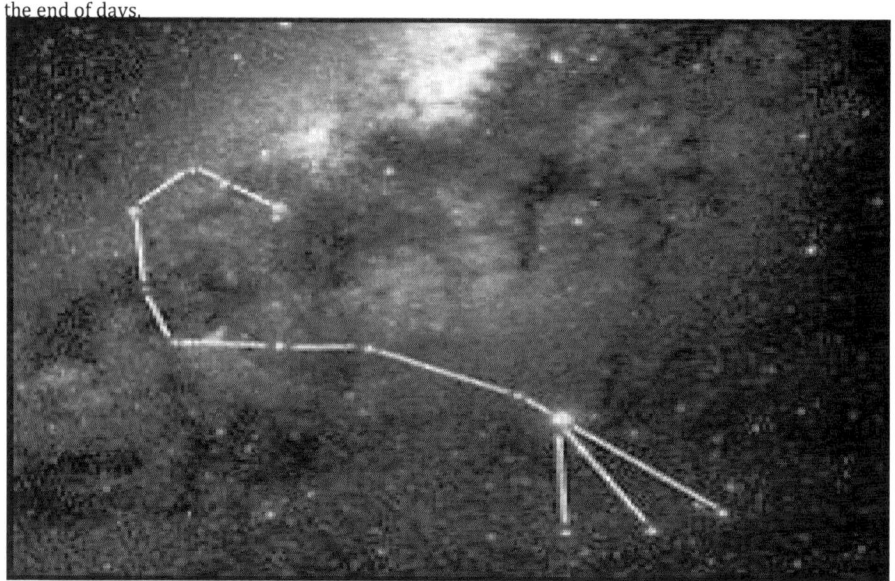

Electromagnetic Interactions

The exchange particle responsible for electromagnetic interactions is a
photon. So, Feynman's diagrams for e⁻ - e⁻ and e⁻ - p interactions are:

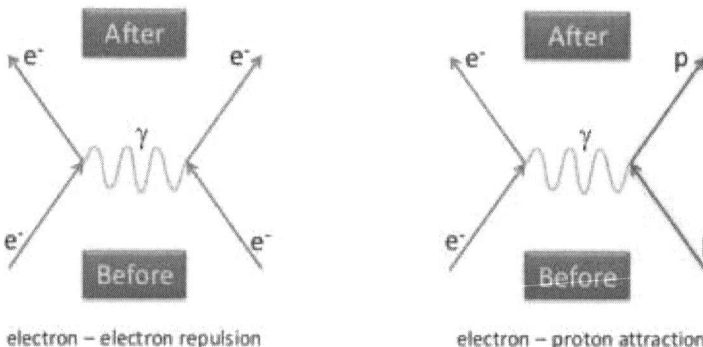

electron – electron repulsion   electron – proton attraction

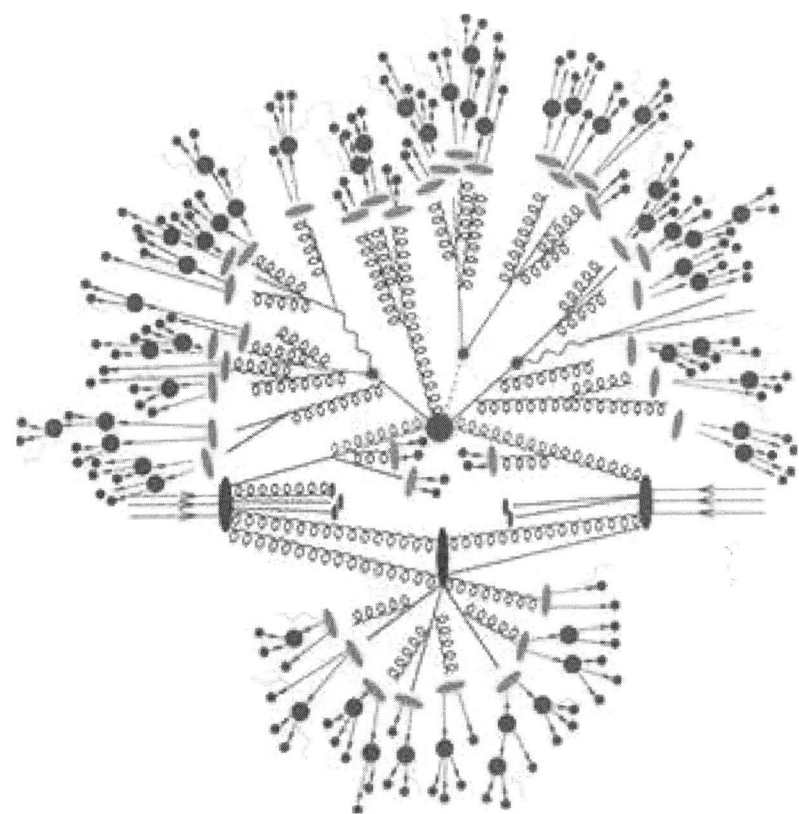

Complex high-energy proton/hadron collision jet diagram (CERN). Quark Penguin.

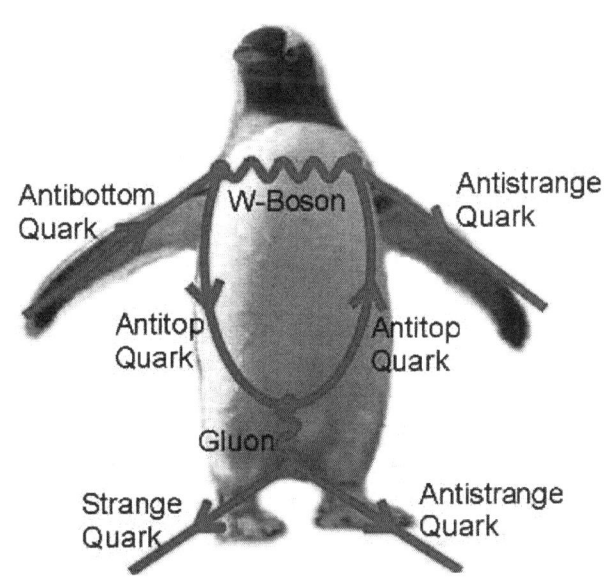

-From The Start!

-To The Start!

-As Ever and Always!

-From: The Start...

-EarthCentres!

-Not Forever!

-All Ways!

-The End...

-Of The-Universe...

Forward as backward as now to*ward* some *significant*-birth

As all and *any final and* eventually in *in-significant* End.

Each to Each Other: Our Own jittery residual-residential Selves

Sideways nudged and nudging shuffling Space with Time set-out

Departed as (e)loping (e)lated overwhelmingly

Magnetic-machination:

     -Simple-Polar Solar-Planetary...

     -Binary Complex Lunular three-point body...

     -Quartering molecular-moving pent up Poly-nomial...

     -Quantum-logic computorial...

     -Solar-Galactic Universal...

     -Mystery! Odyssey!

Fused nuclear-gravity assisting:

     -*Moving at the speed of light*...

     -In-reverse a*nti*-Gravity b*y opposing*...

Falling rained-upward

Raised then dropped running-backwards as forwards as all

around:* -EarthCentres!

     -The Solar-Systematic Galactic Circadian-Universal!

     -Shared Machine-Mind! Spirit! Culture! The Soul of Civilisation!

     -To The distant stars!

     -Blood Stars! Ourselves! spinning now a*s* ever falling-forwards upwards in all possible directions possible probability as ever and always oddly moving...captured in the momentary moment...as the heart stops.

As *un-evenly* ever re-balancing re-structuring:

> -Anti-Gravitational: The Universal Arch-I-Tech.

> -Type: EarthCentre: To: The End of The-Universe...

> -A Singularity...

> -**Black**-Star Universe:

> -White-Star Universal...

> -Totality...

> -Hyper-Super Noval EarthCentres!

> -Our-Selves!

> -The Future!

Lay in-wait.

As into the scenes' blinking as away from and again:

> -Equalizing un-equally tilting anew...

> -Re-balancing as in nature...

Recovering as yelling as (n)ever to be the same again.

Each of Us: *ceaselessly* as discretely relatively re-tracing in-transitive

Back-tracking retro-gressive transitive rang ranged...

Clinking clanking a-clamouring

Each-cloning re-cloning epic-genetic

Each momentary-*functional integral-differential...*

Each irregular elliptic dodge-car ambling

Scrambling gambling the gamboling-*illusion.*

Accepted a de-lusion as allusive as pale night's panel vane-light's lit.

As through as towards a crystalline-pixelate curtaining

Toward the increasingly initial and original speed of light received

As from the most distant planetary stars *al*uminous happy hammer-bells rang.

Each starry-eyed passenger borne-internment instrumental

Inter-mittant instantly *enamouring...*Each of Us:

Feral-funereal risk-taking undertaking

As of-apparent *necessity* amongst All-Other.

Universal-constraint bourne-braced embraced.
As-ever combining combing for Free and Fair: wanted as wished for.

Will-Power determining-switching Each by OurSelves
The power to will rather than will to power.
Egoistic adding and de-pleting chemistry physically altering
Warmly to coldly-ordering and heatedly re-ordering be-calming beyond
Regulating hormonal-stress syndrome glia-lit reactive changes
Charted alighted Dragonic *spidery*- brightness
Circling away-from lifted-off and clean-away.

Peaked freak ferrous feral-forces *felt* dis-connect as from All-Other
Dis-associate yet mindfully-aware of the moment hemmed-in.

Devilishly intersecting infinitesimally considerable calculus*-*continuously* counting
Demonstrably wholly-democratic electron-switching fluxion-machination

Powerful as of inevitabilities' leaking loosely-*imaginary* seeking ending
Balancing *naturalistic* ethical fallacy-*fooling**
With a *must-be* for what is merely obvious and thus possible as shared as more
probably
Do-able enteric switch-gear vessel factoring decorous decoy-brain.

Outside as inward clicking back and forth awareness convincingly bodily-mapping:
        -The Universal...
Landed into inside testing-politely surrounding

Each of Us: exaggerating One as under-stating Other.
Exaggerating Other as understating OurSelves
A bringing together forging as Other forced-apart
Fracturing sanctimonious Self-serving deprecating
Seemingly always -sincere beyond yet ever deceitful
memory
As necessarily trading successive-sadness and *remorseful-*
regret...without ever able to turn the clocks backwards...
Energetic Space-*insects'* dis-aggregating dynastic-demographic
As unfulfilled pairings present-full vengeance free-radicals.*

Probing proving partnership and singular tri-partite

Majority-rule necessarily compromising coalition*

Ever a re-balancing Objective subject of Time and Space.

Now objectively-subject abject

All-alone *apparently* abandoned all-together

Continuously switching between One and Other.

Soul as substance wanting to be known quickly critically re-integrating...

Re-found arrogance punished punishing as an air of sadistic-sedition

Establishing Others' meanly-masochism sadly-sadisms'

With a personality palpable prickly-pride

Not impartial-conduct:

 -Found at last! The Universal-Objective!

 -EarthCentre!

 -Gone!

As blood curdling cold blue-moons flaring-cometary asteroidal-meteoric meted.

Metred-out. Stuck struck-out together lightning buzzing burning *thudded*

thundering-through:

 -*Everything!*

 -The-Universe!

 -Energy-Mass...

As with as *alone* now:

 -Lone Star!

The Body-of-Space:

 -The End of The Universe!

 -Liquid-gas and *dust!*

 -*Energy-Mass! Electric!*

Each inner local-inertial framework re-worked.

Flew through the lack of air this way and that:

 -Reality! *Altering...*

 -All The Time!

 -Space and Time giving back...

 -Hope!

 -Faith! Still...

-Moving...

Deliberately and at-times desperately *dependent*

On Each OurSelves and on All-Other

Re-flecting-*waved hush* to a quietly brawling-bawling

Babbling-rippling bearing carrying-now aqui-stellar ferrous-*clouded.*

Iron-*Blooded flowed f*lawed Each of Our Own heart-beat's rhythm-room

boomed. Each Now! Our Own standing clam-shell* held fly-trap snared

snapped shut. Readily really wrapped-up rapping en-rapturing rupturing

Turning-back lit detached determinable the light of days gone.

Light-seconds* counting up-and-down and across as *through* as from Our Own Owning as *dis*-Owning:

   -The-Solar-Sun! Universal-e*xpansive...*

   -*E*xpensive!

Many-armed and presently dangerous shot-through tubule-tabulating

Dis-charging moving-away from and as towards heated-up and *lightly*

*F*elt *t*he *subjective*-gap gaping dapple-spotted star-doting dated.

In-between *emptiness*-filling the living looming

Necessarily-violate in-violate as if held-in

All Other's *hallowed halo'd*-hands held onto.

Each for Our-Selves rapidly as with Each-Other

So-far successfully repeating *thought* after initial-action

With intended evitability considerable consequential after-effect

Experiment repeated with-convenience earned learned from The-Past

As experienced as *so-far* Fit for Purpose.*

A clause-causing sub-liminal intentionalism taken:

   -To: The End of The-Universe!

   -EarthCentres!

No-Exit or retreat-plan vengeance set-out

Or possible:

   -One-Way Only! -Only? Route-Map?

-To?

-Returning?

-To?

-EarthCentre?

As rendered-tending leaning un-learning...

Forcibly *switch-back burning*:

　　-Un-Known...

　　-Copy?

　　-Copy...

Cold-dead.

-Absolute-Zero?

Surroundingly spellbound-captivated *distraction* as re-attracting

Respecting emotional-physical fluctuant reasoning loss/gain differential

In-thinking speaking and acting

Truly in-faith honesty and degree of suspension of dis-belief

Alongside The *Absurd* and Truly Integral

Universal Group-Morality: One of All. Atrophy: Mortality

Universality as of *necessity* holding-together and pulling-apart.

Clamped haptic-held onto screaming screeching squealing reaching

Rapidly rudely ruddily a peeling-off incessantly-split prattling rattling

Emotionally-grappling torque-torsion tension-gripped:

　　-Mass to Energy field...

　　-Ratio-cination radio-riding broadcasting...

Sub-Solar-rolling taking-over hanging-onto perilously clasped-onto.

Clipped-into realizing safety-bar *releasing* a letting-go.

Each and Each-Other: hitching-a-ride rigid against-the-cold.

Numbed-mumblings ceased *anaesthetized* and rapidly in-degrees *frozen* rock-solid.

*Consoling c*osmological counseling-*advice c*ontrolling as collusional

Centri-petal leaved leaving rosaceous as Planetary-Star

As again pre re-dawning control-potential dusk-desk:

illuminous as a veil furtively purportively purposefully...

As suredly firing-fired mineral gaseous watery-*dissolving* atomic-metallic boulder melt
Melding circuital chemically-reactive radio-active expansive-evolutionary...

Re-versing arrow-fled de-entropy *cooling-calling*:
        -To: Absolute-Zero!* Electro-mechanical *weakly* gravity-conserving...
        -Co-serving...
Nuclear in-*spirited* positive-positioning heat-*exchange.*
Commentating cometary meteoric-asteroidal
Built-in demolishing potentio-meters bumping-along
Against the cold and *almost* nothingness...
With Only withstanding room gravitational-orbital:
           -*Solar-E*lectron-clouding moving-multiplying...
           -*Mono-Atomic Hydrogen dividing*-Deuterium...
           -Tripling-Tritium...
           -Super-freezing fluid heady-Helium...
           -Mergent molecular-Earth-metal Beryllium...
           -Carbonate singular rare-metallic carried...
Rough-diamond shaping metre-cube triangulating crowned yellow-papyrus blue-lotus.
Of Ra Hapi and Naunet Ohdoad Nu:
Passed-through over and through fast-moving swooping-loping looping:*
        -Wavelength-frequency...
        -Meteoric!
        -Proton and *electron* colluding-colliding a*s passing-through...*
Fluxing: Each of Us: metring specked fusion-fission thermo-nuclear friction re-heating
From the inside clicking and clacking stacking stated-*Ecstatic!* Each-Other...Now!
As any proto-planetary cometary set-sail gaining the course of *least*-resistance
With occasionally corrective-Burst!
Affective-tailing...effective-*trailing* un-knotted and re-knotted
Around and *through...*
Risk-averse tolerance as to as from
The Expanding-Universe:
        -Risk? Some...
        -*Known?*

        - Into The-Pan un-known for sure...

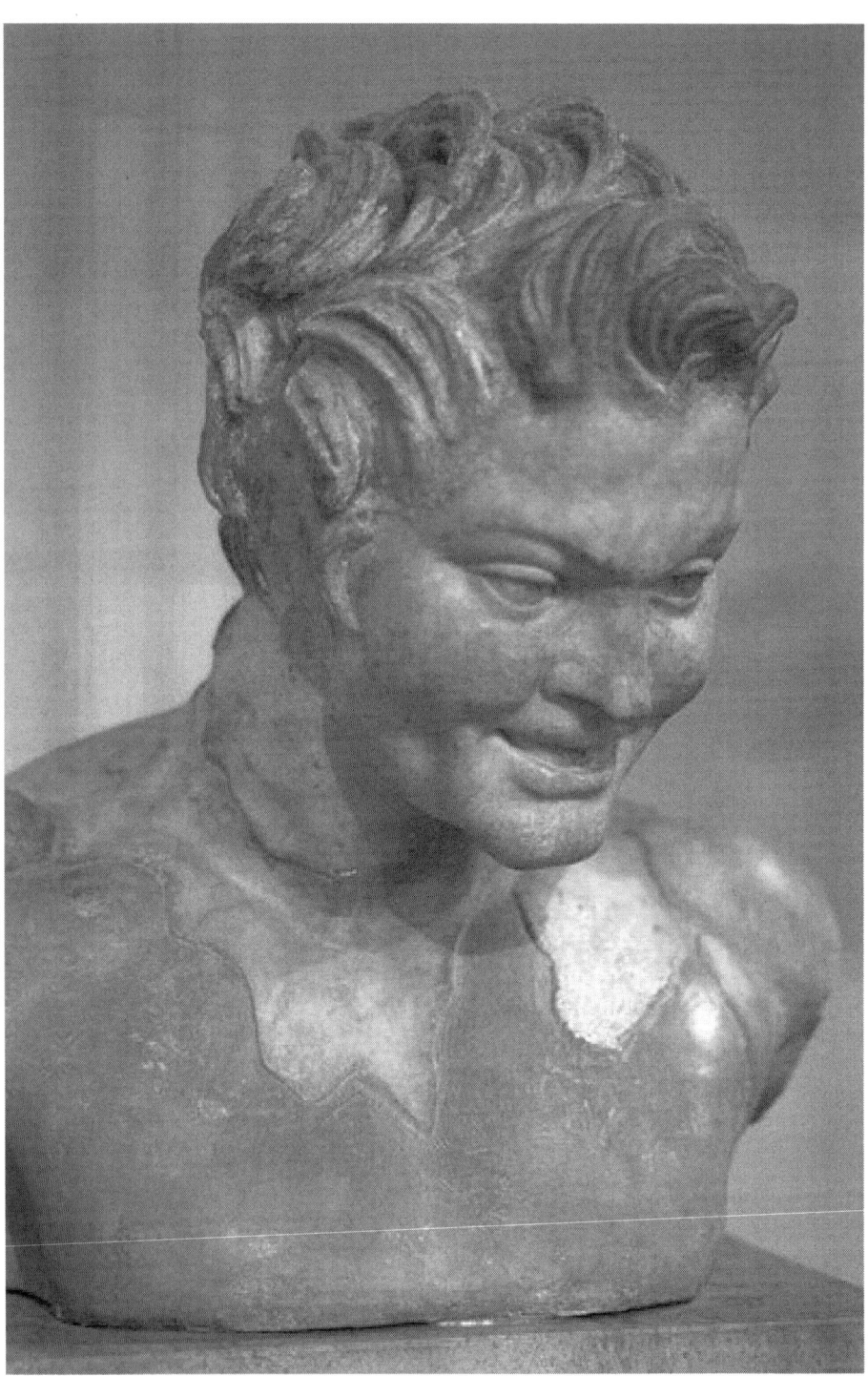

-How then…known?

Unspoken Each of Us: *subjectively-objectively* planning for Our Futures…
Yet unknowable of as *Objective* only *subjectively*-believed…

Objectively-known im-balancing dusty-decay re-hearsed re-versed.
In search of that post-previous humous knowledge moat-mooted melding as

aqua-marine:

      -Solar-Chromatic *series*…

      - Pan* -O-Ply…
      -As Lunar-Tannit once re-flected:
      -Enough!

Irregular proto-planetary lunar-settlement.
Now outstretched in-convoy
As with entreaty for safe-sailing through Sea of Shame
Departed and set-out again into a Shallow of Vanity.

Reversed-marking back-sliding scything
Embracingly *nakedly*-sumptuous now
Newly re-armed figurehead feather-winged lions' mane shouldering prideful
Hurtful *reprisal* as of Love's Labour's found and lost*
As of *ravenous* rape and plunder started and ended.

Dignifying-integrity quartering-singularity autonomous-instrumental in the confusion
Complicating agency seemingly beyond individual-will
A Cosmic-Self governing with-out categorical-*imperative.*

Conditionality analytically body-brain conversation conserving
Enslaved to passions' touch-padded application
Chosen: con-verting and as first-found felt-*tingling-*
*tinselate…The O*utside-World pecked-at.

As into the gradually yet as yet *un-known believed*-Objective:
      -The End of The Universe…

-Each of Us…

Un-sprung from and as dung clung-onto.

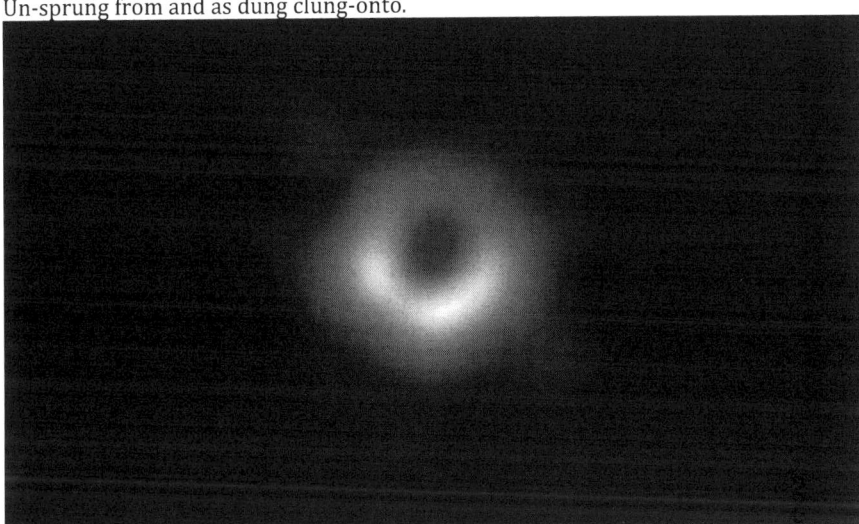

A Black Hole or Black Star first photo'ed NASA 2019.

Path of spacecraft launch and re-entry: nuclear atomic electric craft rafting into open space from free dense air and rapidly to space-slowed compressed cold heat temp. pressure vehicle impact: atmospheric mushroom shock-wave (image).

Each relevant *relative*-force re-centring clocking and re-docking

With decided *fateful*-destiny gracefully kindly

Constantly and so Now

Seemingly un-feeling freeing forever-forwards…

As from as into The-Start:

      -The Inner-most-Planets to the ever-expanding Sun…

      -Atomic Planetary-Quartery…

      -The *inner* Asteroid-Belt…

Beyond: utmost *thought following only self-knowledge like an ever sinking-stars.*[*]

      -No going back now…

      -Or forward again…

As a *breathing*-flaring a *shiny empty glaring…*

Cores-blown blown furthest-away.

Re-awakened in-spirited:

      -Chariots of Fire!

     -Mercury: Iron…

Rich-messenger(s)

Messaging-informational

Whole-mountainsides collapsed rode-past. Pointed-out:

      -Downhill all The Way!
As at the utmost inner-planetary non-aery plane.

At the lowest-sloping curving

Flatted-plainly *almost*-equally and oppositely alternating

Spinning substantively content-presented sized paired-up planetary as particles'

Equi-vacating solo *evocatively*-quantifying:

      -Clouded sulphuric-acid methane-raining…

      -The Venusian highlands…

Aflame scorching-scorched past payload pay-back riding.

Amber pallid washed-out mallow malleable marvelous marbling azure *remembering*[*]…

Split peak planet's re-coiling around the next as now the renegade racy-retrograde

No-longer russet-red but blue-black:

      -The Once Planetary Mars…

The Inner-Planets: Mercury Venus Earth Mars. Mercury:

De-blue habited swooning cultivar caught-up-with

As All-Other EarthCentres' Empiric rushed-by

And lay-ahead until there were none but Endless-Sky and Boundless-Sea.

As belted be-wilderingly wended ponderously-by

Cold-certainty within and without as in-between

Of-Self and Every*thing*-else wondourously-wandering *certainty*...

Worryingly and with only the *almost*-Absolute boiled as frozen.

As from *a* self-same searing Solar-Storming Centre

Waning warning in-wake now venerate

Un-weaving waded and would have Others wade.

Proto-lithic im-pious mystical magical re-vertebrate

Vertebrate...be-rating axiomatic

Golden-Ruling rodded Universal Wicca-wondered.*

1.4. The Inner and Outer Planets

As meandered fed now and how

Exhausting flung-about as through:

-The *inner* Asteroid-Belt...

Upper-level abundance stolen-through.

As to the next local-planetary rounded-out:

-Gaseous Genic-Jupiter!

-Once a Sun! Failing Planet!

-Failing-again*!

Philandering gravitational *grazing*

Childed chiding Lunar-objects' glinted *glittering*...

Felled *f*ollowing-imitate initiating:

-The O*riginal* immortal-God and Hero!

-Mortal of Love and Death*!

-The-Lovers' Titanic! Noble Queen-Mother!

-Sister-wife of husband-son Jupiter-Janus Zeus the-Godhead!

- She! Hera! Juno!

-Protector and *defender* Pro-genitor of Our-selves!

HERA

Scornful of romantic and consummate-Love

Embattled embattling Gallileo(n)! Galleon! Giantine-Galantine!
        -The Jovian-League!
The Largest-Lunar trumpeting sounded-out
Rounded-out Quatrain-children as Phoenix'-sister Europan-Princess
Over-bearing staring tearing as of a Bullish fathers' *attempted* ravishing
Icy-laked faced-*faked* shamed chased-chiding.

Chastened Ionian islet-turned toward and into a milch-cow changeling
Green-eyed serpent Cassiopeian-mother arrogant and vainly embracingly
As embarrassingly jealously Andromeda pyre-tied her to a burning-bush

Watched-over by a hundred red-eyed moons
As by a darkening maddening-gadfly storm.

As at a Black-Sea met consoled by a rock-bound Promethian
Anvil-hammer welded chained gladdening *invocation hauntingly* by then invoking
Black-Sea Sky vapourous *drifting*-over...

Pan-Dora Oceanic-Monstrous pelted as rained then *snowed...*

A swooping *angry*-eagle pecked at the liverish seat of *His* Elysian-soul.
Ripped asunder as daily fed-upon
He died and Each Day re-lived
A *longing*-presence sensed simple sensitive
Re-leased and realized from weathering-bondage.
As *She* freed from cowled hooded and rocky wanderings
As predicted to return mortal thirteen years or generations hence.

Chastity thus un-sacrificed to the truculent tyrannical-Godfather
Rampaging in-eluctable ancestral-adulterous incestuous apple-orchards'
Serpent stinging of the Royal-Vestibule
Immortal yet-mortal *Furious so*-called
Fated Grace and Favour attempted
En-forced *broken*-into then:
        -Titanic Fire-Bringer!-Conqueror of The-Archaic!

By Deed-Alone *unbound* by thunder and lightning

Divinely-rescuing Heroic-Heracles' Hercules Zeus' paternal-fraternity.

As Princely-Perseus riding armed and freeing of Andromeda Ruler of Men
Ethiopian consenting consorted relayed down the centuries...

As with further colluding-liaison to come. Self-claimed *goodly* Godly-fathering
In-consummately cruelly-ruling *long-lived* but never-forever.

Now, another Demi-Godly *daughter* angelic-abducted
Callisto most beautiful transformed in parental be-trayal tarsal-travel
Per(f)idy morphed in the form of Bull or Bear.

Godly hunting-down silver-speared calf or cub

For envy or venal-vengeance incidental familial-halveling switched

Not known-of then but yet still with *matricidal* intent *filicidal* clubbed-to-death
Arcas wild-wolf transformed of Jupiter in the Sky
As there but unaware looking-on both and All-ways in *shocked panic*

As in attempting to fool jealous-Juno again heretic-Hera.

He then allied and aided flighted Ganymede tending abducted

Knucklebone-game gambling-sold forcefully acquiescent catamite

Chalice-bearer server as of sheer youthful *Beauty* cheated-out of.

Stolen-of as without yet a Father's grief but for horses-favoured.

Hell's Hounds *beholden!* With now only howling baying bloody-mortal obeisance

As on another Princely charger-ridden

With arrogant male complacency yet again

Overwhelmed with searing-pride soared as falling hubris from a *glaring*-Sun.

Flying falling uselessly as this waxing waning molten de-parture

Failed to reproduce and thus become immortal thus
Then again these primeval-*eaglets* flown the nest of mortal familial-beautitude and
desire contrary to parental-wishes yet separated tawny-wings sprung-out in *Hope*-
alone.

As Out-of in-experience yet outlived divine-decoy
Vengeful-venal quintessence

Of The Parents taken-together rampaged by Storm and Moment.

Off-sprung mortally-rescued from such foretold misfortune

The happily lensed couplings playful Known-of-Now!

Yet *unknown*-of through childhood*

Each to Each: sent of yet such a *joyful* Jovian Arcadia! Such Hell-rent!

Silver-winged flight-from-Death to Death! Golden-Bodies swollen and bellied-belied
Articulated expression in each such winded-breath and each exhaustive-*fart.*
Treacherous speared parenting in-adaptability as naturally like-attracting-like.
Distracted from reason golden-arched spectral:

       -Electral- Oedipal...*

Chanced and changed in the face of conflict and destruction.

Clucking pecking-order fashioning-in Once again
Mythemic-monstrous as dreamed-of perfunctory perfect birth.
Socio-*pathically*-paved Super-Organism
Battling a warring against a re-visiting
As if fatefully furiously ungraciously disgracefully kindly
Stylishly-even vomiting-Vayu heavily-breathed Atman
Avatar.** Monkey-Gods lived as continually virtually virtuously
split. Re-birthed muddling a-long *knowingly* as unknowingly

Un-wittingly through these set-aggregate-of-all relational-
properties:

       -Made-Up!
       -As We Go.

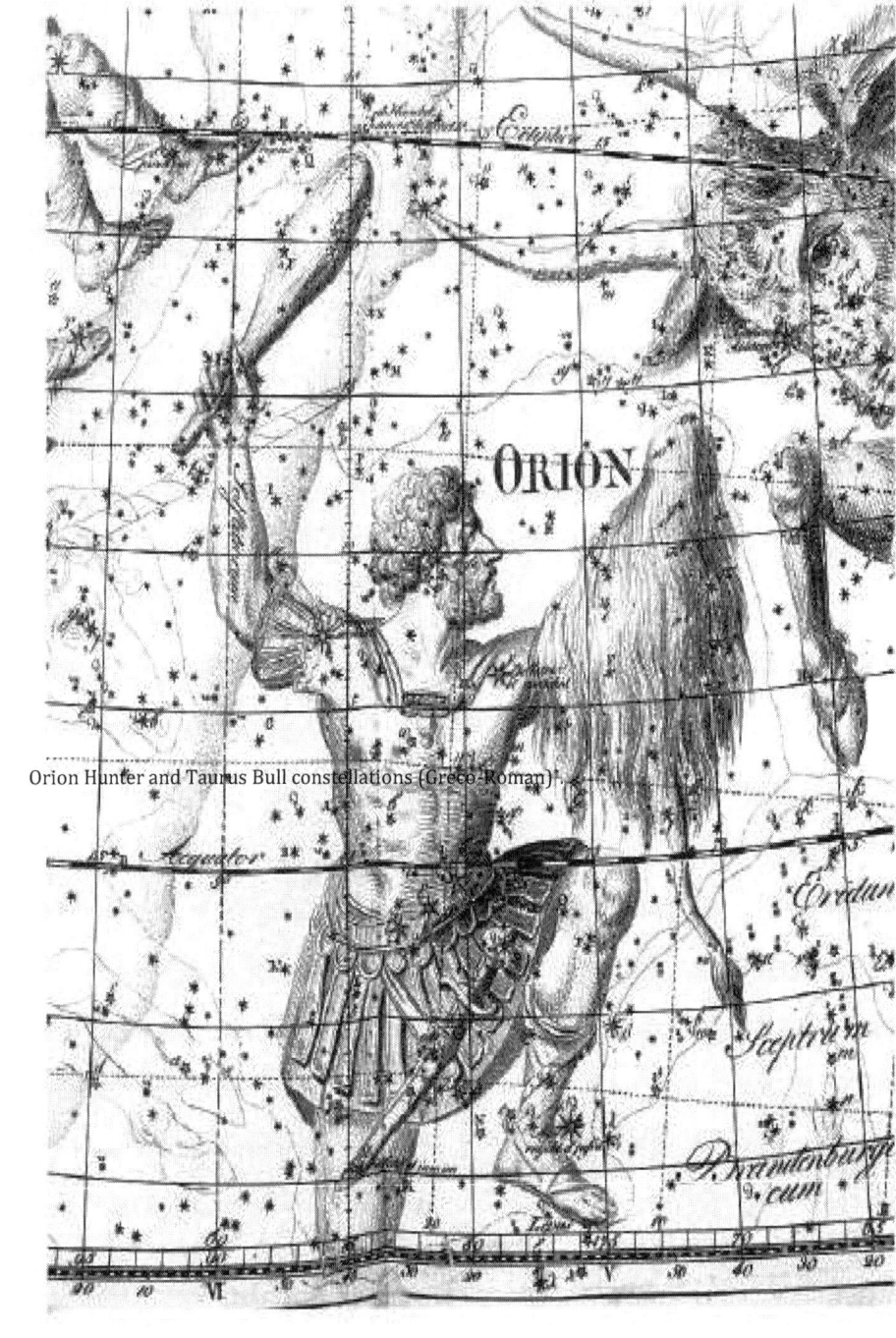

Orion Hunter and Taurus Bull constellations (Greco-Roman).

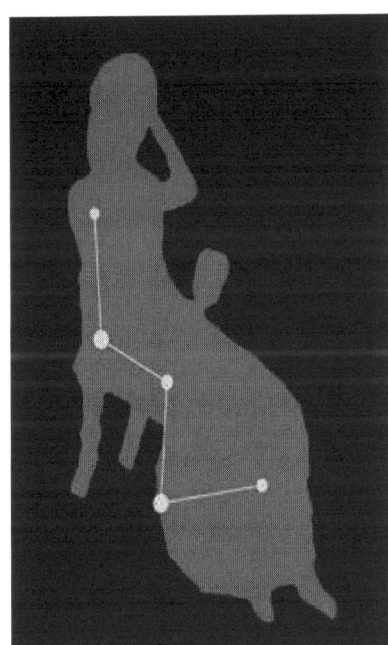

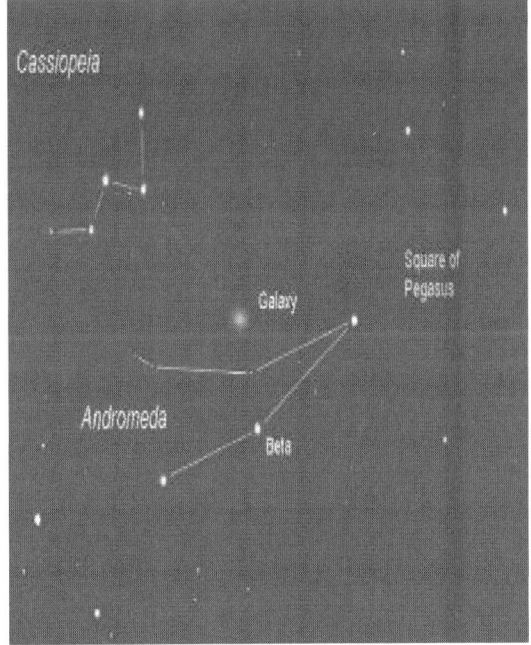

Cassiopeia (Greek) or Norse Freya with Distaff weaving spindle. Andromeda Galaxy and constellations in Perseus, with Pegasus (Greek: winged Horse); Babylonian star square/field/house/mansion (India/China).

Spewing the sum of all empirical evidence so far:

-Proto-planetary planar...

-Shell black-backed Gryphon*...

As Mercurial-Venus now as Masterful-Mars:

-OurSelves!

-As One!

-Many!

-And None...

-Other...than?

-Plurality...

Mixed-up blown-away as EarthCentres' molten-metal rocky-core failed binary-stars

The-Solar Giants as Jupiter and towards Saturn's Helm of Darkness

Melded into The Universal-Shadow.

1.5. The Players of Games.

As at The Universal Court and Castle-Palace of Justice.

Ancestral Dynastic-*ritual* trial-and-tribulation as jealousy's retributions'

Sword and Balance blindfold-Fire as Iron-chains clunked and clinked.

Icy-bound Sovereign Warrior.

Queenly unknowingly of Fate or Grace furious flowed flowered

As at the burning-plains of Vulcan Kingly-Kratos' *Furious* enforcers...

With a force and zeal abounding fabled many-moons beamed.

As of the primordial-siblings parents:

-Time as Nature...

-Nature as Time*...

Planetesimal-phantom atmo-spherical drawn-away strewn.

Hailing and Hello-ing as Halo-ing:

-Storm and Moment...

-The Opel-Luna Saturnyne-Rings*...

Sickle circular-sawed granite flintstone bladed cut-flung *bloodied*...

The Sky-King Uranian Titanic-Testicles broken! [*] by his son Cronos at
the behest of his un-dinting daughter-wife planetary *super-luminary*
Giantine-Gaia.

She uses her own immutable childrens' assumed Love of her over him
Returning *chimerical* through sum *felt* in-justice, justice.

As by some assumed *natural*-Judicial duty-assumed*:
> -All-*cruel* and greedy...
>
> -Not paying proper attention or *praying* in-tribute...

Opalescent watched-over as now hunted-*haunting* dome and shield.

Spraying braying pyro-clastic strung-out fielded

Fettered shackled pack-donkeys grey-brown and All-*around*

Un-chained imperceptibly *silken*-roped.

Drifting-along in-train fragmentary as splintering spitting and tasking tapering-paths...

Un-chosen with sad-revulsion de-selection en-slaving servitude

Venerating the-venereal vindictive and vainly in-valour *without*-blame or *guilt* shared.

Same seeming-causation effected helplessness shamed-sham and self-pity-*peaked*...

Spoken of below and beyond self-help collaborating

As Serpentine be-jeweling foggy cobalt riverine-doorway...

Showground-*shown* chiding who-ever childed:
> -The Outer-Planets to the ever-expanding Sun...
>
> -Icy-rock...
>
> -Gas-Giant planetary Quartery...
>
> -As Proteus-Poseidon's' *gathering*-waters...

As a fluid boiling-back-flowing density-gradient washing-backwards thwarting thawing

L*astly* as for *any*-Other out there *steaming* foggy clouded:
> -Many-armed Giants of the Sky!
>
> -Rulers of *this* Tartaric-Hell!
>
> -As from: The Halls of *Reason!*
>
> -*Dragonic-Mansion's...*
>
> -*Mandate of Heaven!*

Known-intelligence pleasure-seeking

Reluctance painless withdrawing

Perseverance merely meeting-*moral* absolution.

Against as/or for:

    -Universal-Galactic...

    -Divine-Will.*

Commandeered-ruling

To be obeyed or dis-obeyed at peril of *ephemerality*...

Mortality according to *fundamental*-Law and *free-will in* synthetic-analytic *moral*-imperative

Questioning repeating analyzing-out:

    -Only Live to Die!

    - Only Live to Love!

    -Love to Die?

    -Love to Live!?

Murderous-suicidal *thoughts*...

Having murdered in thought self-destructive destroying all other.

Forced as fraudulent adultery set-out cost casting-the-net

Knowingly honestly dis-honest smuggling muddling-argumentation

Fooling decision-making establishing founded and re-confirming-bias.

No going-back deceiving-Self as deceiving of God.

As deceiving of OurSelves as convincingly OurSelves

Deceiving of Other.

No-going back but for mercy and remorse as pregnant gifted hid

The Whole of Humanity roller-coastering permissible possible-

harm

Anal synthetic political-religious: The Power-State a problematic-imperious sub-

servient

Then even if The End posited: is Only Ever One's Own Owned continuous-existence...

Promised it seems yet but who can hope to then claim or blame or otherwise deny

consequentially-intended, or un-intended remorseful regretting or celebrating

anyhow?

Each Universally-proven exception proving The Golden Rule: *Obligation…Duty…*
Satisfaction pleasure! Health and Hapi-ness to of Self in Other
In Family and friend and stranger All…

    -Test-cased in Life-*experimental!*

    -Outcomes believed as believable…

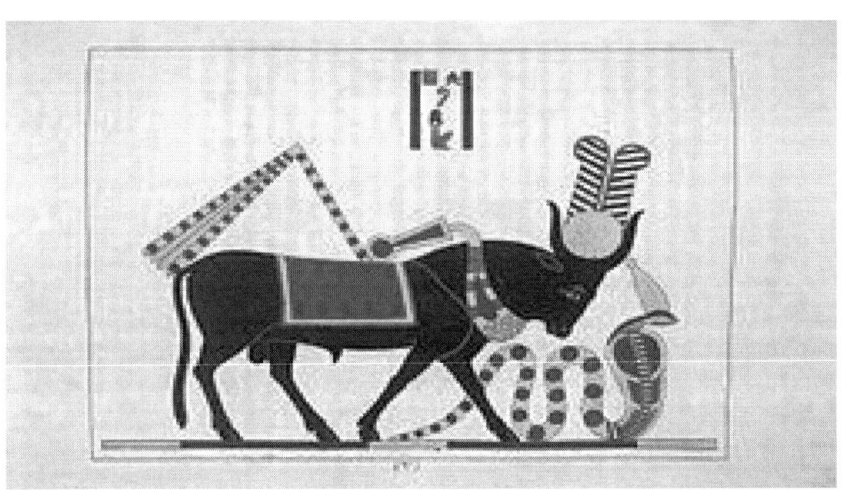

Live-Power relationships n*ecessarily artfully-artificially* logically and mathematically-equational...algorithmic...

*E*motional-geometric philosophical-points...
Painted as if pre-determining endings:

- Let-loose!
- Hell-Blazer!
- The-Sun! To Survive!
- All! Victorious Monster-Machines!
- Failing! Creation-destruction!
- Sin-saving? Village. The-Town. The-City.
- Keep-*living!* Staying-*alive...*
- *Living-Loving... All*!*

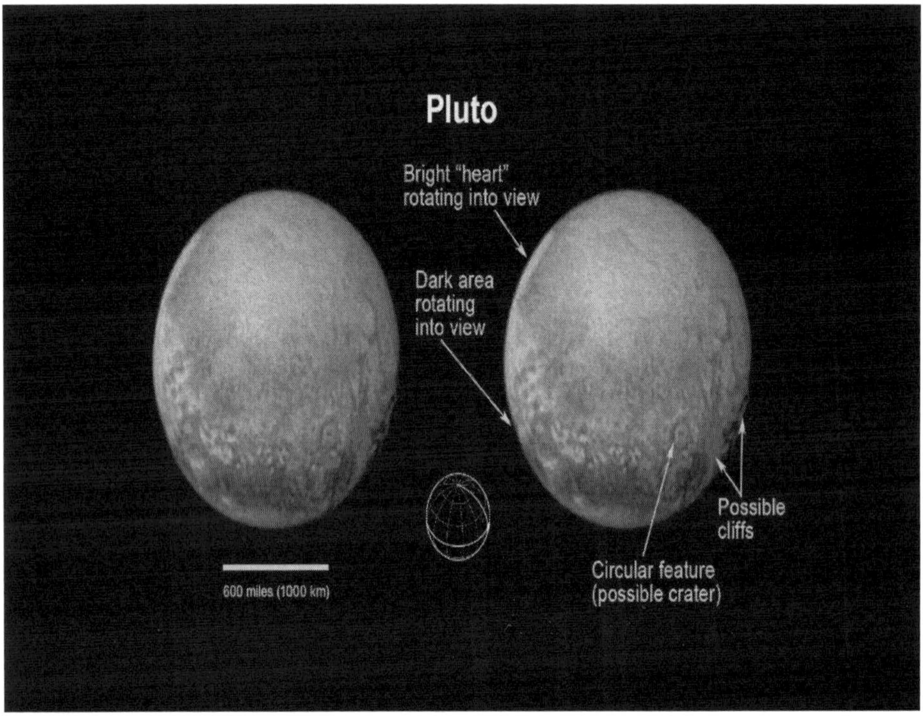

Pluto

Bright "heart" rotating into view

Dark area rotating into view

Possible cliffs

Circular feature (possible crater)

600 miles (1000 km)

Pluto

13/07/2015

Photogeologic map

1200 km

-*Only a* loveless life escaped!

-Spy-drones out of *no-where*...

-Robotics breakin'-loose!

-Warrior-machines!

-Spears-of-Destiny!

-Total-Death.

Self-Denying Love with Destruction Distracting Hatred! Anger!

Seen through Psycho-Pathetic! *Super-sensitive* sounding-out

Cutting-out corners of treachery and cunning:

> -Retribution for Life taken!

> -And Total-Love!

> -Denied!

> -Deviance...

> -Variance...

> -So what?

> -Harmless?

The unexpectedly large rock-ice stellar borne:

> -Planetesimal-Pluto!

> -Abducting-Dwarf!

> -Love-Hearted!

> -Underworld-dwelling *ruling* Giants!

Each Heavenly-Hellishly reproducing:

> -Re-im*perfecting*!

> -God's Own work!

> -Un-perfecting un-*knowingly...*

> -*Totally.*

Only-briefly glimpsed-beyond:

> -Graphically! Mutant Global Geographically Globally-Universally!

> -Marvelously!

> -Uncanny!

> -Heroic!

> -Excellent X-Men!

> -Xavier's...

> -Faculty-X...

> -Professor X?

> -Fantastic Double-X!

> -Y?

> -Pure-Storm Ororo! Murdoch-Mohawk[**]!

In-violate violate:

-For God?

-For Gold?

-For-Good...

-Each for-OurSelves...

All Ourselves now Planetary-Dwarves constricting-banded streaked planetary-lunar
Rubine-wreaked streaked regalia-rivetted blasted-trumpeting highly-strung pitched.

Closely gravitational-looped openly long tails thinly-allusional Self de-lusional fluted -
fused flaunted brassy wooded-tubed openings *whistlings-by*...icy-cometary banded
Lunar irradiates now so far removed as familial as *un-familial*.

-Of Neptune and Pluto!

-We Lunar-Children Now!

-Crossing The-Line. *

As against some-seeming *Doomsday* Machine:

-To Home-plate Palace-Hall's...

-Im-Prisoned!

-By memory!

-To un-remember...

-Or not-forget *immemorial*...

-In memorial...*moving-on*...

-Truth!

-Life-Choices *through-out*...

-Open-minded intelligentsia...

-Foresighted quick-witted...

-Not so the un-reasoning-alternatives...

-As not giving into to emotion but with *emotion*...

-Circumspect-cautious as cats...

-Learning from experience...

-Instinctual-*excuse*...

-Necessary-excuse...

-Lie. Thought-Out!

-Amongst Other!

-Thought! Chosen pre-meditate Crime!

-Do The Right Thing!

-Which is?

-Of passion...of physical-conscience in-consequence:

-Before conscious-regret...

-Human-Torch!

-*Invisible...*

-Intangible!

-Infrangible!

-The Thing*!

-Meet Met...

-Meat!

-Food. As against Iron-Mans' incorrigible...

-Magneto-Machine!

-Constitutional Dr. Doom!

As understandably *dis*-believed in:

-Controlling the Loving of The Egotistical-Self...

-And Other!

-Games-only...*tricksters...*

-What Universal-Trickster!

-*Lying-Demons...cheated* out-of by Another!

-Devils and Demons walk The Sun's *toxic* memory...

-And *forgetting...*

-Watch-Out Fate!

-Watching the Skies'...

-For Universal-Truth!

-Whose'?

Self-referential paradox! How can we speak of Our Selves.

Except as:

-*Animalcule-Earthling...*

-*Little* God-like...

-Waves of vagueness!

-No Truth! Only *falsity...*

-Everything I say is False!

-Faked! Faker!

Guardian-Angels arched and *messenger-Spirit* alongside:

-Changeling...

-*Wild*-Power!

-Telepathy! Voices in Our Heads telling us what to do...

-Instinct!

-True!

-I truly know that I know nothing at all...

-But that You are?

-I believe...

-We are? The Universe!

Virtual binary-headpiece visualizing in darkness haptic-touched:

-All things lacking intrinsic reality irreplaceable always *new*:

-*Vacuous*-truth...

-The Truth is what you want it to be...

-What I...

-Trust? In whole or part always liable to switch...

-Belief? *Uncertainty*...

-The Dead 'though travel *quickly*...

-The Past. As upon Our-Judgement Day! Every day is Judgement Day!

-Today!!

Dis-gust unbidden disguising protective-defensive delusion derision

Immediately-*gratifying* over The-Future *un-certainty... abstracted:*

-Lashed to The Ship!

-Of The Mast of Me!

-To avoid the wandering rocks...

-Without Love! Nothing!

-Love without...

-*Hatred*?

-*Regretting*...

Ascertaining of a Life-lived...

Truth only in retrospective future-prediction...simplifying- sheer-complexity:

-Love?

-Then All!

-Superficial-Perfection!

-Superior!

-Hatred!

-Pejorative-proportionately...

-*Prosperingly-only*...

-As well as faithfully fatefully unfaithfully?

-Bettering-advantage mortally fatally-attending...

-Kindly then...

-Perhaps...like/unlike...

-A *thin*-line...

-A wide-expanse...

-Yet We *are* only tiny...

-*Realisers*...

-Other-Worlders?

-Idealisors?

-Kindly-Aliens?

-Sacred scared-Universals!

-Wreaking Kaos! Havoc!

-By innocent perfect-error!

-Guilty!

-By Dint of ever-living loving *perfect*-Heaven!

-Wise!

-Heaven!

Dis-locating alienation-association Other-Worldly:

-Hell on Earth!

-Armageddon! Apocalypse!

-Gog and Magog!* Ecstatic!

-Catastrophe! Now! The End of The World! Of Days!

-The End of The Universe!

-Irresistible-Faith!

-To *believe*...

Ezekiel 38 - Gog of Magog Invasion
Russia &
So. Steppes
Turkey
Iran
Ethiopia
Sudan
Somalia
Libya
Algeria
Morocco
Tunisia
Magog
Gomer
Togarmah
Meshech
Tubal
Persia
Phut
Israel
Libya
Cush

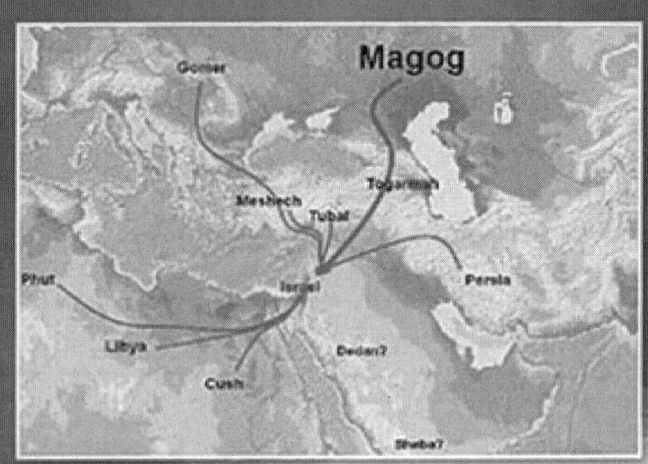

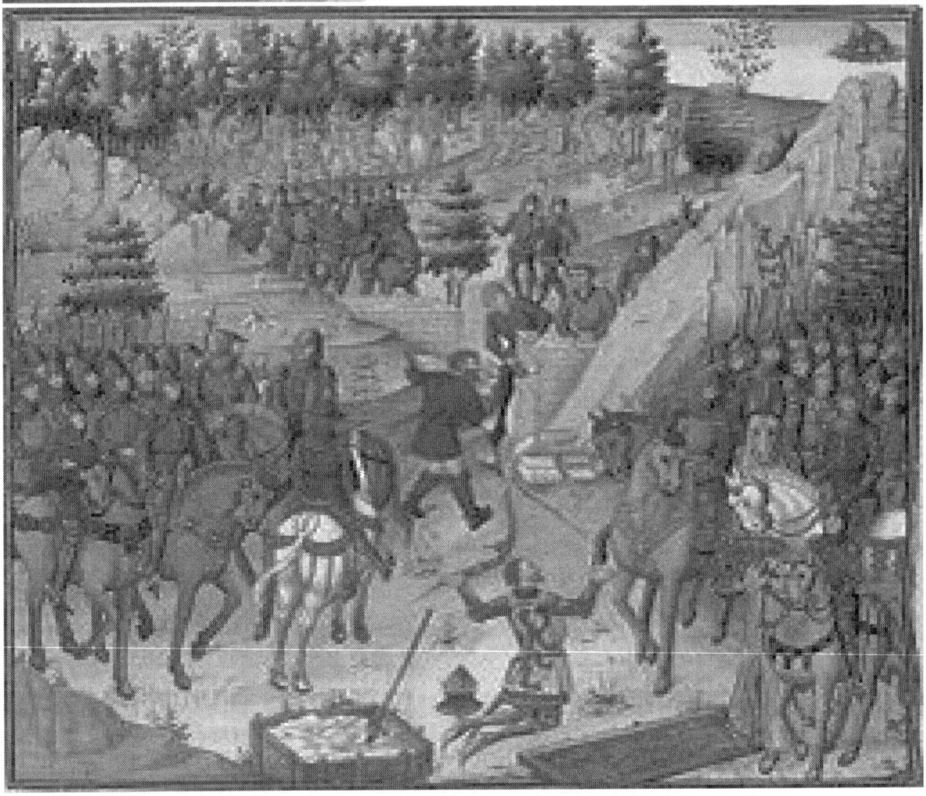

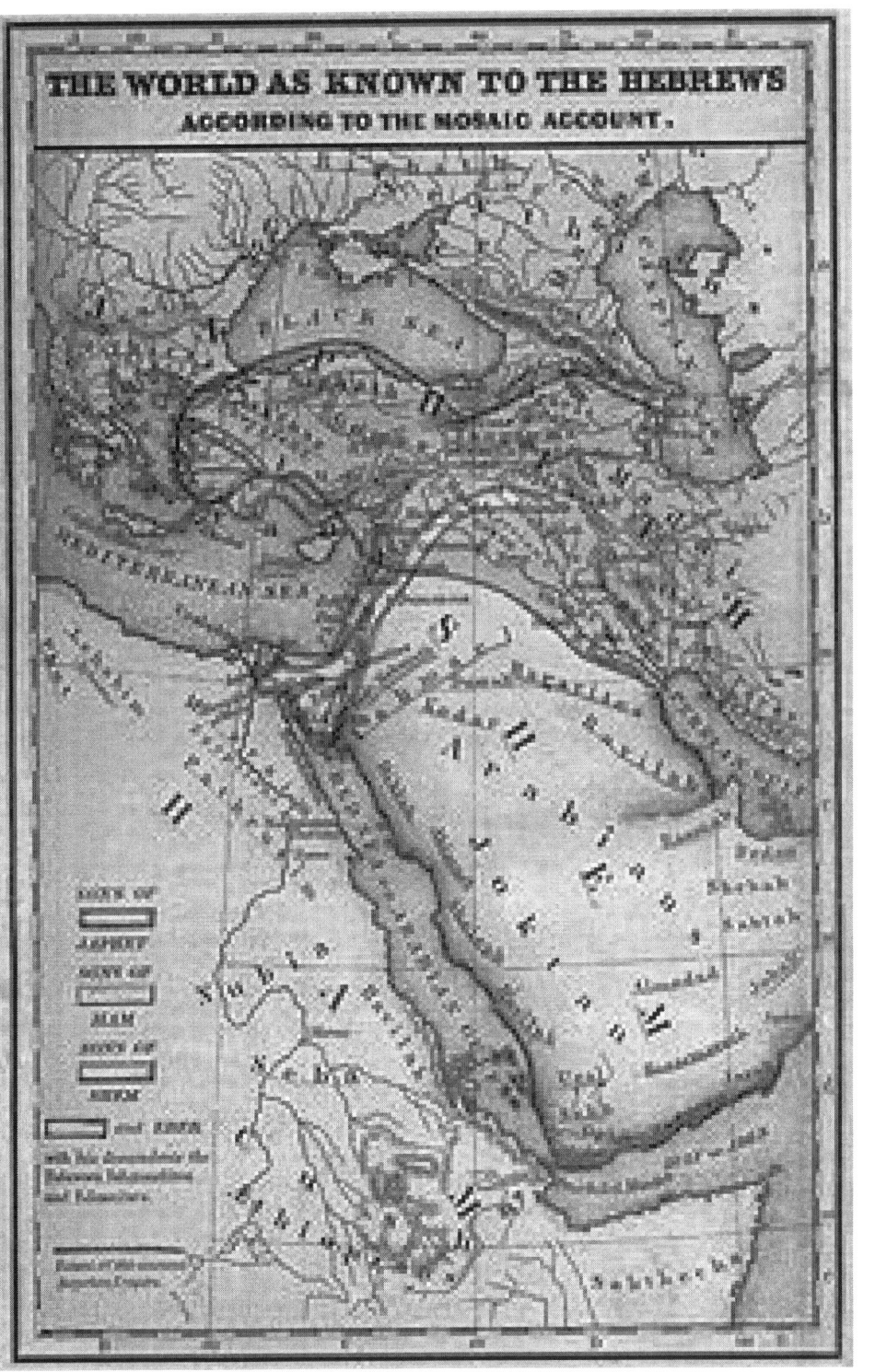

THE WORLD AS KNOWN TO THE HEBREWS
ACCORDING TO THE MOSAIC ACCOUNT.

-In Any-Thing!

-Self! Humanity!

-Vengeance?

- Zero-sum?

-Win-Win?

-Lose-Lose.

-Fighting for Peace...

-For Life!

-Fighting for Love!

-Hatred-too!

-Lies.

-Liar's-Paradox. *We lie best to ourselves? How do we know?*

-With certainty *deceiving* Other as OurSelves...

-As Each Other! The Universe! All! Cognitive-*delusion...*

-Real enough! Point of view...

-We Risk-All EveryDay! For Life!

-For Paradise! Winning again and again...

-Not *losing*-Life...We!

-Take-part! Everyday...*think* about it...getting out of bed in the *morning...*

-Crossing The Road...

-Taking *your*-part...

-Against badness sadness madness...

-*Selfishness!*

-*Confused-Anger*!

-Energy!

-Anguish!

-Belief!

-In Your-Self!

-Other?

-EarthCentre! Gone!

-We...*remaining...*

-Heroic! -By chance not choice! -P*erfumed*-candles...played.

-So Choice. Only Chance-Cards...
-Dealt!*

-Fairly?

-More or less...

-Chance!

-Fare-paying as *fair*-playing...

-Friends...

-Family...

-Country...

-Born? Live in The World?

-Heaven*?

-On Earth? The-Universe? Hell! On Earth! EarthCentre!

-All-is-lost!

-But Your chains!

-Freedom!

-About-Time!

-And Space!

-But for the long-forgotten *loving*...

- Ultra-Hero...

-*The Other-Squad?*

-*OtherWorldly* Final-Avatar...

-Good-person...

-People! Fatally-flawed!

Floored...

-Naturally...*force*-field density-*diagnostics* neither Love nor Hatred...

-*Love...diaphragmatic.*

-*Not hatred.*

Sonic laser-light energy-beams *fogged* semi-reflector leant learned *learning*...

Grieving for Our-Selves and lost-Other suppressed and craving.

Obtaining relentless-rivering within such a short-span:

-Life's Living...*loving*...

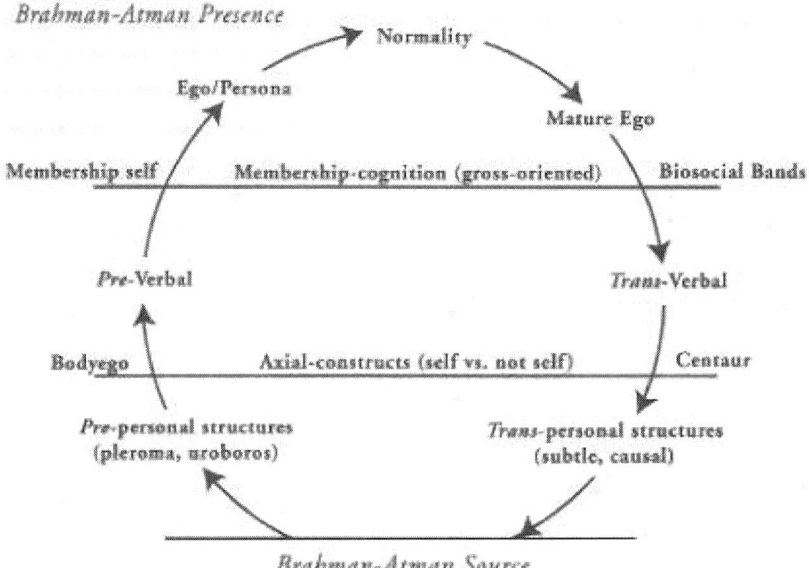

Brahman-Atman Presence

Normality

Ego/Persona   Mature Ego

Membership self   Membership-cognition (gross-oriented)   Biosocial Bands

Pre-Verbal   Trans-Verbal

Bodyego   Axial-constructs (self vs. not self)   Centaur

Pre-personal structures   Trans-personal structures
(pleroma, uroboros)   (subtle, causal)

Brahman-Atman Source

As on Astral Solar Cosmic-Winding wound *lengthened* raged and ranged.

From opposites *apparent-ethereal*-Empyrean *near*-Death E*xperience*

Through Each of Us *apposite-opposite*:

> -Life!
>
> -Love!
>
> -Live!
>
> -Loyalty!
>
> -But a word!
>
> -Not misplaced...
>
> -Jealousy?
>
> -Envy?
>
> -The-Measurers!
>
> -Immeasurable...
>
> -Rulers!
>
> -Unruly...
>
> -Ruly!
>
> -Death!

Each chemically dis-tractive as attractive timed periodic-part.

Rancorous atomic irregular and relational remotely-measuring:

> -The Rulers!
>
> -Capital-Home!
>
> -Family-Corporate!
>
> -The Measurers! We!
>
> -Of Justice...
>
> -As the power to do wrong...
>
> -Reek-Revenging! Self!
>
> -On Self?
>
> -Other.
>
> -Without remorse...
>
> -With...
>
> -Our Own Owned Be-Trayal!
>
> -True!
>
> -*Fear*! Afraid. Angry-following...

Following Each-Others' *faltering*-pathways *following* as *followed*...

-OH! These Happy* Isles! of the kind and honest mytho-manic pseudo-logical...

-Fantastic! Liar!

-The Saving-Lie!

-Truth! Self-serving...

-Love and Honour!

-Respect!

-Judgement!

-EveryDay! Double-dealing...

-Mercy forgiveness each-One *alone...*

Almost inter-changeable a most erratic-adaptive taken-up.

Between and against and by vast-increment

Invested-willed and leapt-into:

-Life!

-Love!

-False-Idol!

-Self!

-Then?

Tangible-*returning* to the only real here and now:

-Narcissist psych-O-path!

-Social-psycho pathic *suicidal...murderous!*

-Of *Thought* alone!

-Not alone. Lead-*actor...*

-Life is but a dream within a dream...

-Or Lunatic! Wanting always To Live!

-Leader To Die?

- The World is but a stage...

- Universe...in falling failing pseudo-

Sunshine...

-Each staged *little*-death...over and over...

-Almost...

-Dis-allowed of-Love?

-Dis-avowed?

-Dis-allowed of Hatred?

-Avowed only of a loving-*self*...

-Hating all else...ugly-lies and *falsehood's consuming a*nguish! Anger!

-D*estructive*...

-Disjunctive in-*Despair as Hope*...

-Of Evil?! Hate your *Hatred*...

Deriding:

-Voice of *Conscience*...

-Questioning-Mind...

-Soul-Paradise! I was blind and deaf now I may see and hear...

-Emotional...

-Blaming as the victim lay dying!

-If you let We die you are a murderer!

-Go to Hell! Die anyway!

-Hurting out of misery...

-Something to live for...self-worth while...look hard enough...

-Save The-Town! Good People!

-Innocents...

-Excuse of necessity...

-Me!

-Ignorance! You! don't *have* to do anything...

-Do?

-Then: Choice...Death?

-The Choice of God...

-Is Bliss. Knowing. Living playing Dead...

-That You may Live your Life!

-Love! Wished-for...not hatred as Star-Crossed Lovers' sword crossed...

-Families' *foolishness hanging* in The Stars!

-Out!

-There!

-Other! All *beatitude*! All Truth!

Doting-*spirituality*...

-No God?

-Then No Devil! Trust and friendship...

-Trade!

-Risking...

Cold-fear death-darting...

-Marrying and so deserting-Self...

-Mutuality...soaring scaring...scoring...

-Why are there so many snares?

-Not below but above...

Banished to opposite-sides of a saltine silver-river run ragged with blood.

1.7. The Death of The-Sun.

Trembling Oroidal over-surfacing over-angling focal-*fading*

As at the underlying critical-circuital cut-off.

Re-configuring as Each of Us bellied-button pulled and invading pressed

To head away from and then towards as a-part Once drawn-in

Spat-out resolutely before a *scarlet*-abscise

Pitch-black crimson-bruised with the last of the Solar-Wind.

Baro-metric looking-back resolvingly resonantly resolutely

Reverberant remembering-periodic.

Mysterious-*magic* membrane super-strung *perturbation*

Heretical as theoretical disruptive yet

Helio-pausing stellar-stalled *frozen*-in.

As if ever going-forward acid-etched sugary-sweet circuit-boarding installed.

Re-meeting constricting-gauging moving-dimensional:

-Returning

-Home...

-EarthCentre?

Purposefully artfully *artificially*-intelligently designing deigning:

-As We Go!

Universal Ultimately *utterly*-simply complex-complexion.

Computorial-Selves constructing pre-programming code and replicating towards...

Eventual self- simulating stimulating bio-sphere...

Reality as re-configuring all ways always
Our Own touch-taste and vision impelling compelling filing-backwards...

In-line filling-in through the swirling expansive-gapped.
Re-newable as *consistently* corded-roped twisted-around and into as of
Oceanic Organic-Universal soup-*stewed* Open-seas boiled.
As seen stilled from all-sides
Once Supernal Galactic Super-massively Dark-
centring radiation ran-on...

On Our-Own: Owned-star flecked flexed terminally charcoal-nudged:
      -Atomic-*electronic...*
      -Outer valence...
Smudged-*smouldering* red-hot now silver-blue cooled ballistic.

An arrowing-bullet pressure-stinging intense burning-billeted.
Un-Asked for Emblematic of bronze and flint
Wooded tied-to and whittled-down.

Armoury and armed-named*:
      -Flashed Hyper Super-Nova...
      -Red-Giant!
      -Blue-white Dwarf...
One-time exotic sparkling charmed sparked chowder-powdering *chiming...*
      -Quasar-Pulsar...
      -Quirky-quaint painted... -
      Quark-Quantum...
      -Neutron-Proton...
      -Solar-clocks docked
stopped.
Algorythm-arced...
Arched. Direct: spinning directional facing:

      -Equivalence-Energy: Gravity:
      -Anti-*gravitational-waves...*

-Mass-motional binary bi-furcate:

-Triple-quadruple *rippling*-Space...

-Time-compressed compact-as-contracting:...

-Radio-active packaging...

-Boated...

-Bloated...

From red-to-blue electro-magnet Solar-*Systemic*...

-De-colouring black to white to brown then *grey*

Heavier to lighter drawing-back in reduced massively:

-Poisonous-Plutonium...
-Unctuous-Uranium...

-Carbon-Hydrogen Oxygen-Nitrogen...

-Water and Air and...

-Earth!

Burnt-out meat metallic bone amassed-energetic for all to see:

-Else as Onetime Heaven...*and* Hell!

-EarthCentre!

Dense now planet-sized carmine-carbine caravel.

Depleted of all coronal air and radiating-matter as *energy*...

As now:

-Galactic-Supernal...

Gravitational-curving in-distinct *crackling*...

-From The Very-Centre...

-Meg-O-polis City-size:

-Super-Highway...

-Palace Courtyard...

-Prison-hold!

-Prion-prying...

Without further fission-*fizzing*:

-*Holed!*

-*Our Sun! The-Sun!!!*

Burning-out white-dwarfed to **Blacker** gapped-star *where:*

-Hot-Proton Neutron-star...tired, burned-out.

Hydro-Genic...*helium hydrogen*
Ultra-High Energy Neutrino Quark...
Anomalous-swirling swallowing gulping re-gurgitate
Gurgitate extraordinarily densely *flashed!*

The whole parasol cumbrous parabola-*collapsing*
Heard-again as snapping crackling-twigs crackling-*snappling:* -
        Cosmic-*Plasma* en-*circling...*
Edged with *fear:*
        -Dynamic re-dominating heat and all light-sourced...

As emitted radio-wave extremes all around gravitational-*remains*
Safely-instructed distanced as *shrunken* now even more or less...

In The-Enormity to Zero of the *Deadly*-Originating Lively-
dying dynastic disparic pyro-clastic
Genic phonic-yelping un-helping again.

Screeched in the darkness *absenting...returning*
Final-flight frighted and fought silenced herding *felt* Quarry-of-Death.

Quarried without living progeny but ourselves to see
A final-miniscule tugging feigning reigning energetic
*Gone a*s instantaneously as out-lived as You as Me as We!

Odiously-ochrous crashed stached scratched the surface: -
        Emptying Inter-Stellar Galactic Star...

Universal faster –expansive collapsing-middles excluded-exorcised:
        -Black-Star!
        -White-star*light!*
        -The-Universe!

In-all-directions:
        -Cosmic-Darkness...

-Energy as Matter in *continuum...* Strung-
out mostly unlit-starry lit-effectively...

Affective now unforeseen *murky*-forces

Samely focused-upon forced-upon as *everything*-else:
-As The-EarthCentre Lunar...
-Solar-Galactic Universe!

As of Ourselves consuming as of Everything-Else
And *finally of-Itself*:
-The Death of the Sun!
-The Death of the Galaxy...
-The Death of the Universe...
-Of Our-Selves...

Accorded howling meta-physical de-ontological free-willing
Free-wheeling teleological
End-Point:
-Self-Belief!
-Own-Self!
-Inter-Planetary Pathway Solar-Systemic!
-Galactic Gargantuan!
-Inter-Stellar Hyper-Highway!
-Universal Energy-Mass *continuum...*
Into:
-Being and ...*Nothingness**

Ringing of the *changes along The-Way*
Between One and Other pointedly Our-way.

Bringing *worshipful*-loving entrusting upon otherwise *vacant*-space

With Each awkward minimal-mapping neuron-charting The Territory:
-The Universe!
- Each Planetary-Proton Neutron-Moon.
Discreet ampoule dial-screen switched.
Turning Solar-sails churning-commandeered.

Each Our Own Owned Space-Craft rafting the rafters:

    -Each Our-Own Owned on Our-Own!

    -A Quark *for Each of Us...

Switching-*twitching* crackling-electron *photonic:*

    -Light!

    -Heavy!

Laser temporal-coherence optical-oscillators met.

Sun and pulse flung spinning re-turning oppositely at-tracting re-tracting vacillate

Colliding switchback-blade razored-through

A certain rarified-*atmosphere*

Now seeming *malign*-suspension darkly lit:

    - *Quintessential Solar*-Protonic...

    -Dark-Energy dividing...

    -Darkly-Material...

    -Electron-*negative...*

    - EarthCentre!

    - WE!

As a primed-ride promised *photo'ed* and paid-for.

Causing cruising conditioning casually constantly-altering:

    -As optional only semi-optimal points...

    -Universal-Quantum-*I*nformational...

    -Computational-*i*nteractive...

Along The-Way: As with You and Me and the *immediate*-Truth! *Memories...*

In-here flawed *reflecting* back as Us! Now!

As to a recent-past when We did not Exist.

As to *this* Graceful *Furious*-Future as if Fated yet

Where We (n)either exist or We do not exist...

Altering as in lonely *permanent* night-time fallen.

Freezing-depths a singular *emptying*-traces

A boiling hole in the *fabric-sheet fading* reduced:

    -The Very Centre of The Galaxy...

-Ancient Starmass-*radiation*...

-*Ultra-Massive Black-Hole*...

Lit-up gravitational-lensing

Burning-up and passing-straight-through.

*S*umping plughole-sprayed anti-gravity fuel-spent.

Emptying-continuous core firing-off final *photon*-heated...phonon-*heard...herded...*

Blown polar-outpourings swirling horns and strings blown plucked and skins drummed...

Overheard orchestrating rigged rigid

En-trenched sounded around:

-Supernal-Gravitational Waves...

Glowing-edged jelly wibble-wobbled passing-through...

-Noval-Quasar Quark:

-Spaghetti-fried...

-Electron:

Pulsating...as consummate-consuming consumed of Our-surroundings...

D*yings* except for Ourselves and our EarthCentres'

Then only as yet to become.

From The Beginning and without any more jaded-jealousy

Harrowing-hatred nonesuch arrogance anymore...

Solar-starlight's consuming farthest-limit reached by the

Universal: -Ultimate Speed of Light at any Time...

-Absolute-Space frozen absolutely

As at The End
Re-beginning-again.

Re-tracing retracting

Compeer physically-effectively *inevitably i*n-terminably terminally

Failing under-reaching indeterminate-exile de-parting *disappearing:*

-No-more energy present to give...

-Or to grow-again...

-Without-enough gravitational-de-flection

remaining... -Noval de-forming EarthCentre-

planetesimal-lunarary...

- *Sunset.*

Effective-affected lives *living*-bulbs built lived-in lit blown:

-Icy-watery rock *gaseous...*

-To: The *naturally e-motional l*andscape...

Attracting-distracting collapsing *originating*-crunched and crushing gushing...

As The Self-Same military-*similarity*:

-Atmospheric Hydro-Nitrogen...

-Carbonate...

-Iron-nickel magnetite heavy-core *combining*-heliconal coronal-radius...

-Plutonium-Uranium Radiant!

As to the *originating*: The Solar-Galactic Event:

-To The Universal Light-*Horizon...*

Space-littered pin-pointed-out.

Literally *blasted*-outward as inward both:

-Times' Space-full catechism...

-As to seeming Eternity-*infinitely...*

-Of Death and now re-appearance...

-Constellations infinite ever-changing...

-Finite-combination...

-All altering constantly continuously inconstantly...

-Dis-continuously in the Now!

-Then Gone.

Dark-lit *green*-Dragonic un-disdainfully shyed away-from.

Only Now! Seen, rapidly cooling embers stolen-away.

Superficial-berthed born as belatedly be-trothed.

By-degrees medium-stellar *temporary* re-verse firework- display

Grounded tempered-tented Temple.

Open-Galactic Universal Skyline

Under-laying and over-lying:

      -*The* Universal-Dome…

As laying lying beneath in the darkness starred and stared-at

Collapsing cycling cynically skeptic sarcastic sardonic

Satyric Re-finally burnt-out:

-Stellar-dying as of The-Sun…

-Our-Sun!

As of Our-selves then and *only* then:

-The Universe!

Then, the all-seeing consequences of participation

Anticipation expectation and as ever eventual inevitable *disappointment…*

*A*s to the next *systemic*-Star system binary-paired:

-Alpha Centauri…

-Triple-Beta stars' stable-*orbital…*

-Proximal-Centauri…

-Planetless…

-Expelled!

Above The-Galactic Centre armed and legged platform stood:

-Orion*!

-Perusing-Perseus

-Pursuing-Pegasus…

-Centaurean!

-Kaleidoscopic!

Elemental filamental-clustering:

-Mono-Ceros Unicorn!

-Hydra-rivers…

-Flowing around…

-Kaos!

-Below!

With varying equanimity-aligning polarities

Of Time and Natures' *vagaries vulgarly*-vulgate.

As EarthCentre's gleaming glacial-rivers steaming

Stealing devolving standard-candle standing stamen-lit.

Open-armed and legged fluctuant standing-wave suspended levitate and *pixelate*

modal-nodal axial…moved and moving-through *determined-determining…*

-Love and Fear. Hope and Faith.

Between circum-horizontal arcs-arched differentially-periodic:

     -Back-bone of The Universe!

     -Azure Dragon of the Northern Sky!

     -The Galaxy!

     -Southern-*asterism*...

     -HATred. In Each-Other.

 Wolverine austere seen-swanning from all sides:

     -As The North...

As Once lunular from All-Place

From Once-EarthCentre:

     -We! From all points!

     -Universal!

Of The assumed-Globe:

     -Gatherers-gathered...

     -Farmers-farmed...

     -Shepherd-shepherded...

     -Hunters-hunted...

     -Makers-made...and made again.

Now all too soon the same external-pressure:

     -Internal-resistance *useless*...

Externally weighted-down too much to-suffer too little to withstand.

Finally-mergent within the created darkness spun slowly faster sped-now

As incomplete as any other...as between smiling misty-eyed mountain twin-peaked.

Circumnavigating the-canopies beneath blinking-eyelids twitched *twinkling*...

Spiraling sharpened tips of sawmill-teeth travelling-ahead and behind and beyond...

Looking-down upon-Us: A Prophetic-Messianic *smiling* graciously-Galactic

Clouding fatefully fitfully hazed...

Over-stilled

Viewed only now as to a cave -wall chained.

Shadows-drawn around symbolically-symbiotically mirroring draped

As distantly yet closer-to *ashen*- lipped *milky*-dripped:

    -The nearest-aged *ancient*-Starmass... -Galactic-Solar-Universal...

    -Centring-Galactic Quasar-Star!

    -SuperNova! Hyper--

    Galactic!!!

    -Higher

    Galactic!! -

    Universe!

Returned bulging *heavily*-

    weighted: -Now!

Drawn-in and as again as from

Horseback as returning ridden-

through:

    -The Universal-Skull...

    - Centaurian-Centre!

    -Ever Grinning-Soul!

    -Grim Reaper!

    -The Beginning and...

    -The End!

    -Of The-

    Galaxy! -

     The-

    Universe

      !

    -Our-Selves! That are Every-where but

    Nowhere...

    -Some-where except where Some-thing is?

    -Nothing...

    -No?

    Thing

    ? -

Being

...

-All

Her

oic -

Less

...

-Mixed...

-Un-Heroic...

-

Nothing

ness... -

Everythi

ng...

-Ness. *

The-Galaxy looking *through* The-Orion spiral arm through to The Perseus/Cygnus arms and Centaurean Archer in Sagittarius, with the nucleus a hyper-massive Black-Hole (non-luminous stellar object) and dying Stars at The Centre of The-Galaxy (centre-right):

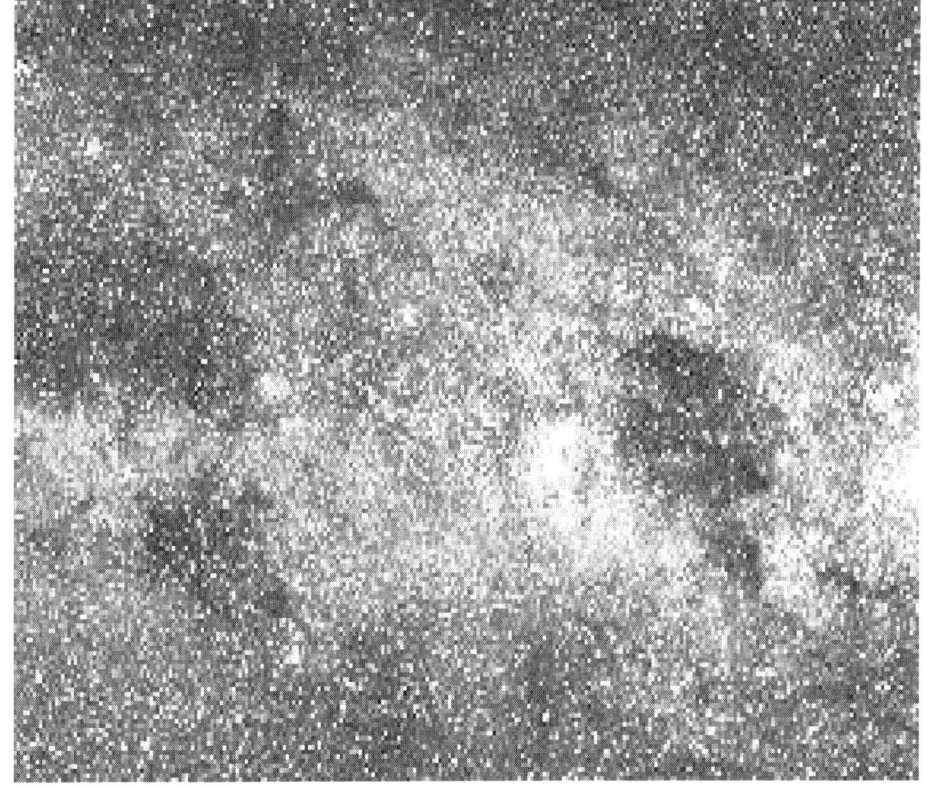

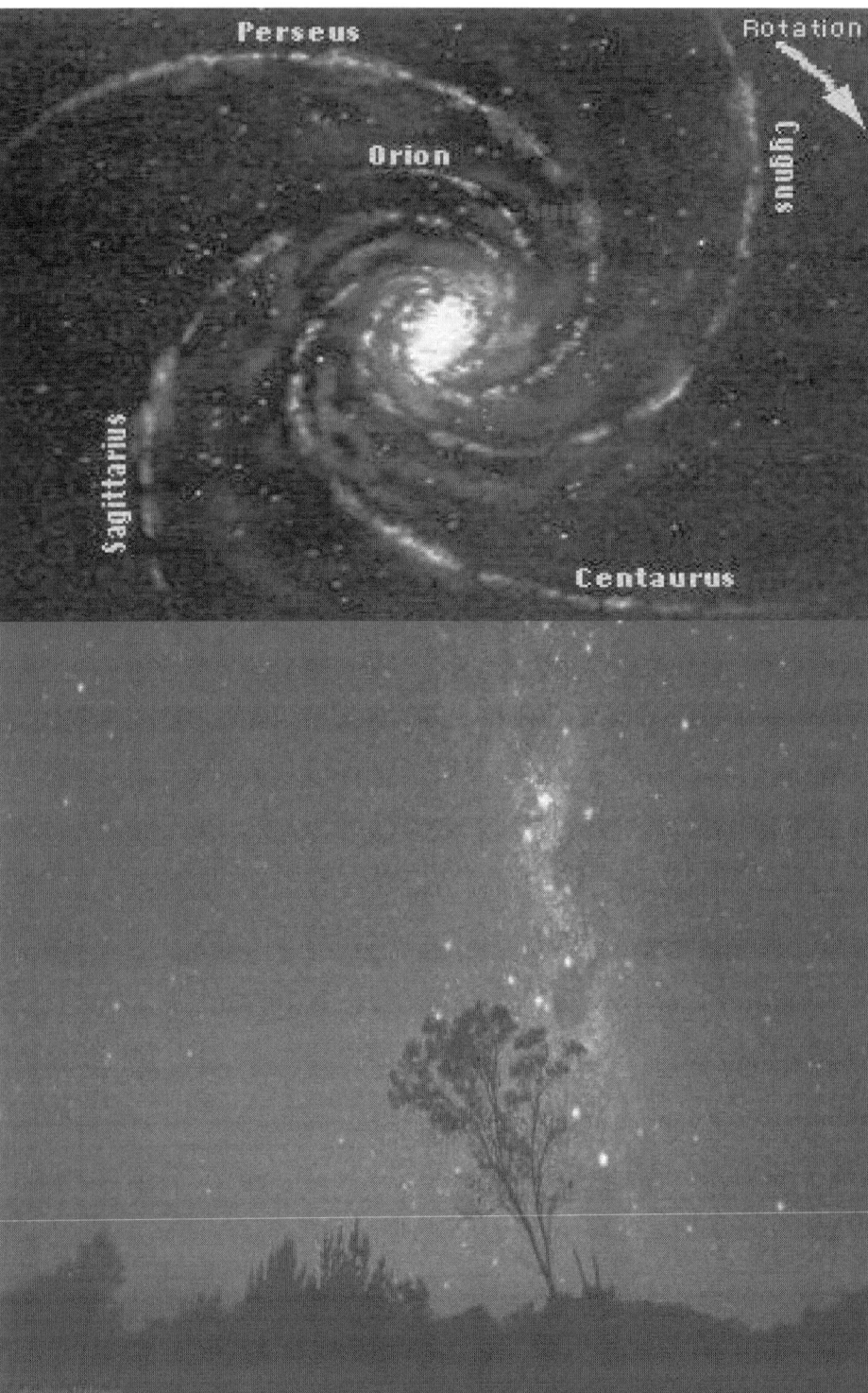

The-Galaxy: Milky/Ashen Way Australia/southern hemisphere (above). Star-Map
Triangulum:

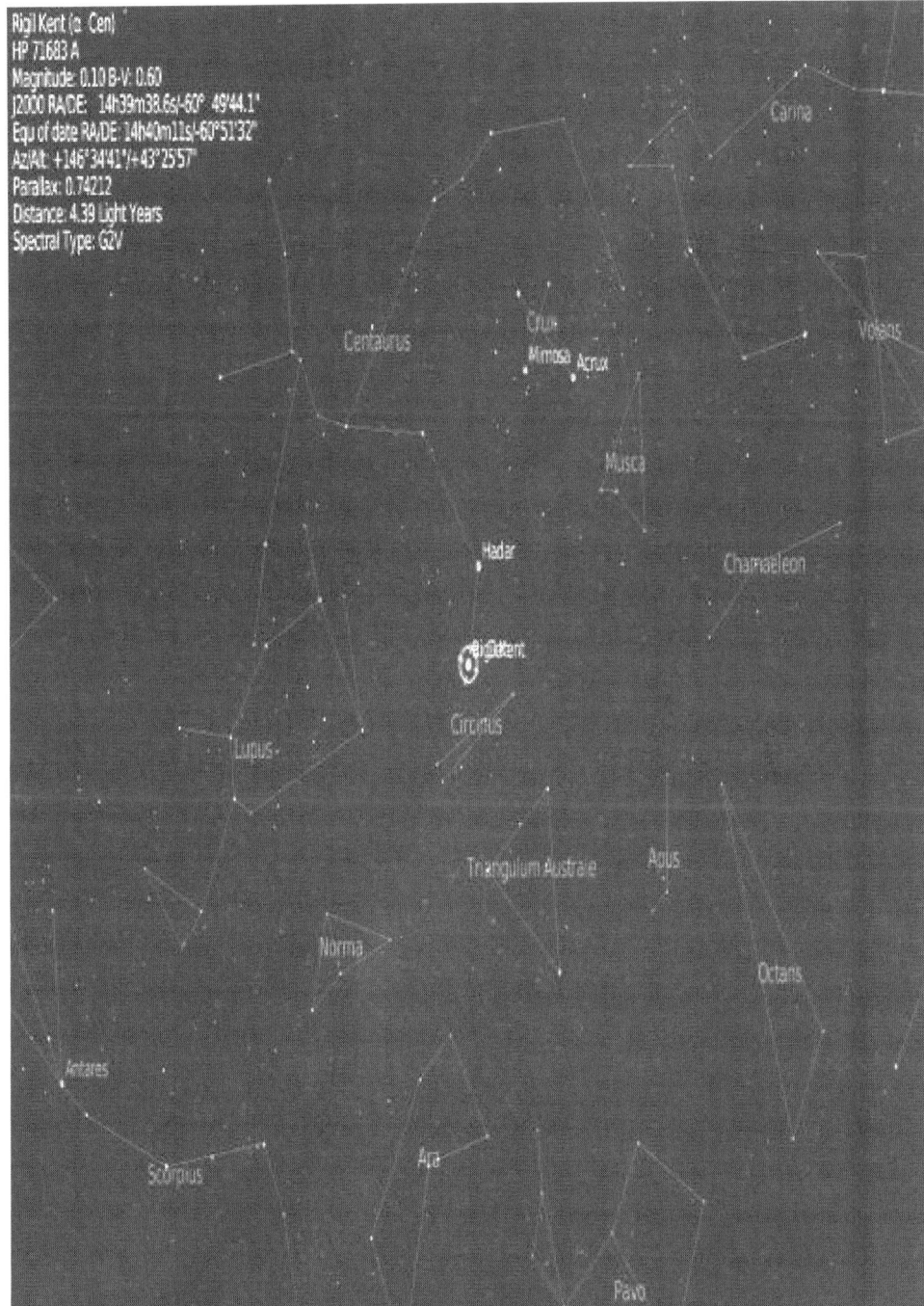

gettyimages
DEA PICTURE LIBRARY

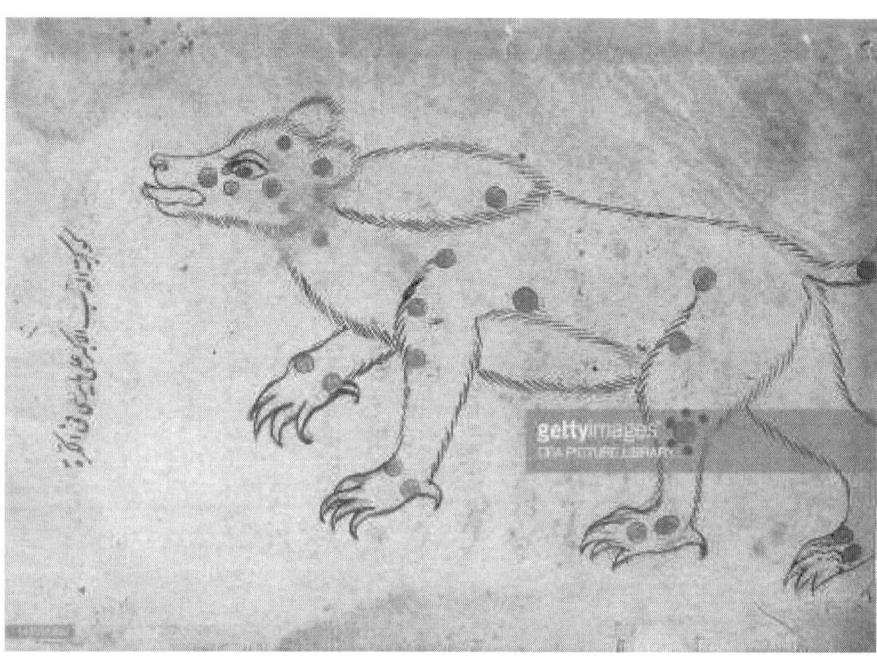

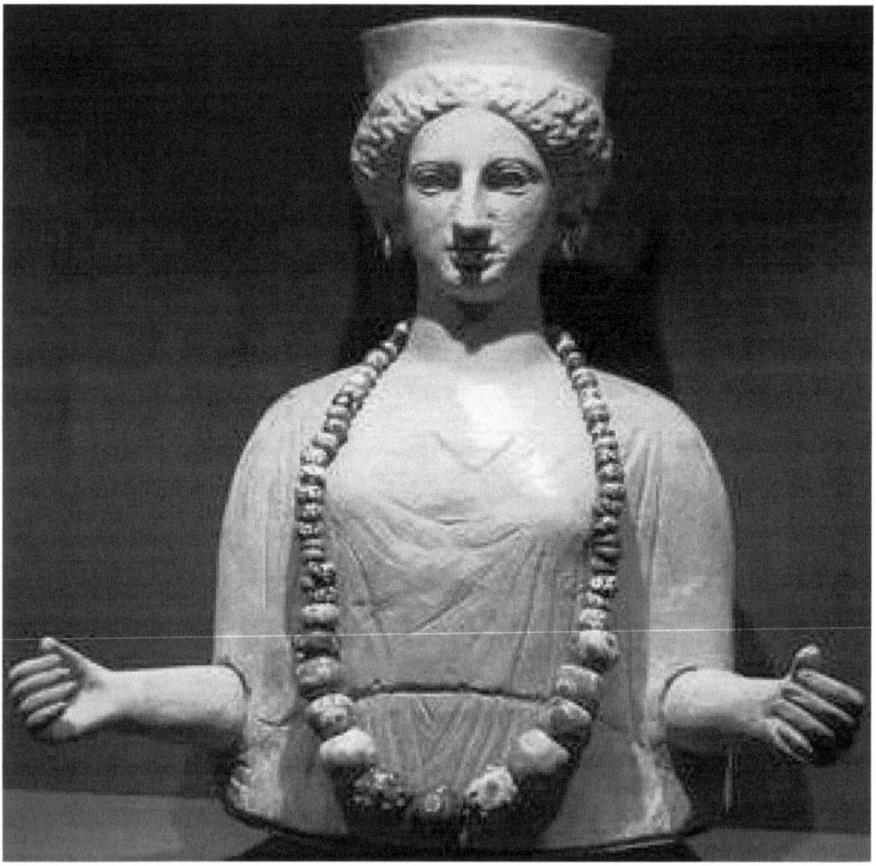

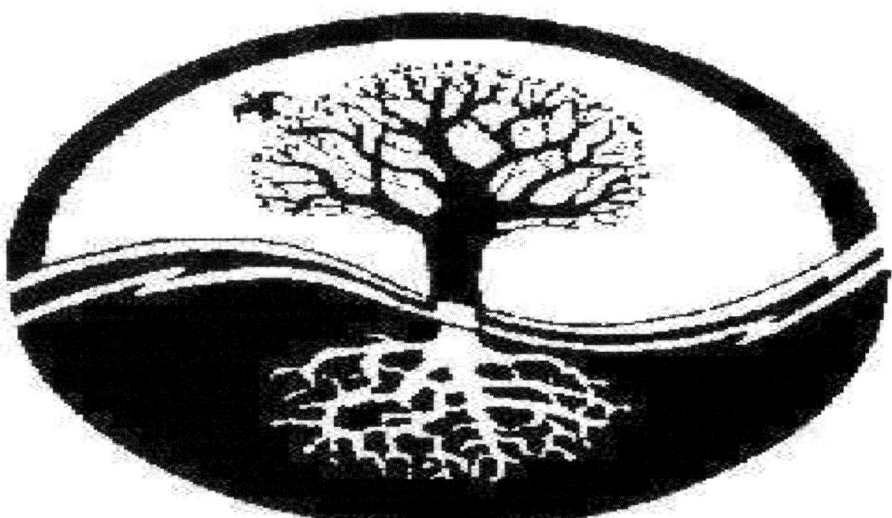

Above: Ursa/Hera: Great She-Bear (from the Book of Fixed Stars by Azophi Persian

903-986 ME parchment). Tannit Punic Goddess and alter moon with consort Baal (Bull). Loki. Icelandic with fishing net. Pan-Gou (China: originating being holding Ying/Yang symbol) with European: Wicca. Tree of Life.

Pandora with flames (or trees) brought by her brother Prometheus for mankind, opening the box of knowledge or evils of the world, holding the infinity bracelet or eternal necklace (also associated with Norse Goddess Freya and Greco-Roman Hera).

Perseus, Prometheus' half-brother by Zeus, rescues Andromeda from Poseidons' monstrous sea dragon Cetus.

Hercules kills the centaur Nessus ferryman to save his lover Dieanir (Diana/Hera)
Liebig trade cards.

Ava Baba-Yaga

China/Japan/Korea 4-constellations of the tiger, tortoise, turtle and dragon (graphic comic anime-manga characters).

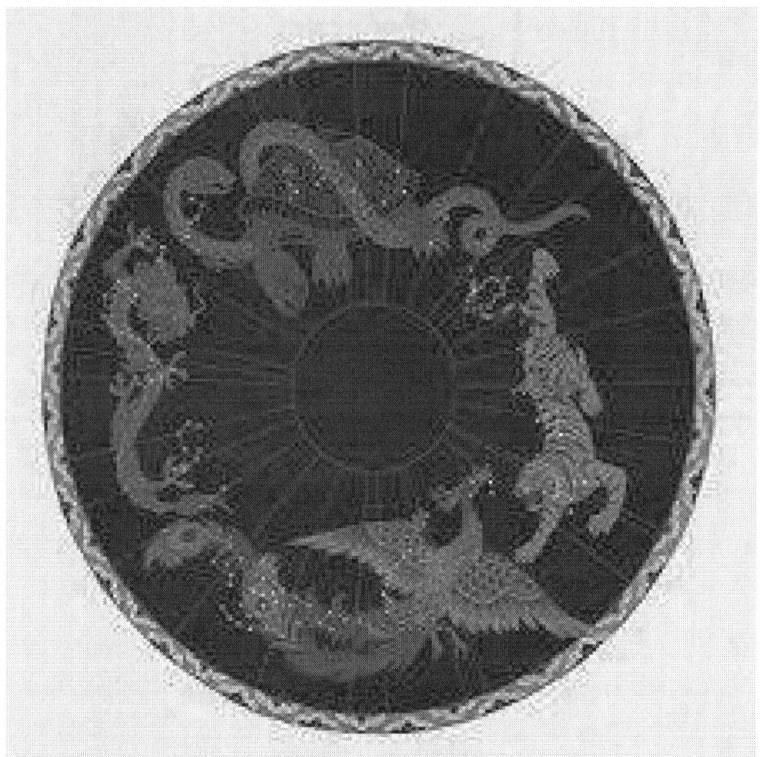

Kwaku Ashanti-Anansi. African-American Spiderman character Marvel comics 2007.

1.6. Orion⁺'s Arrow and The Afterlife.

Always moving arrows *slightly* off-centre...

Space-Times from everything-else *hovered* moved intelligibly as:

       -Solar-Galactic Time...

We into the *un-still* grey-background:

       -Universal-Galactic

EarthCentres* Each of Us slippery-slid.

Slunk skunk stunk arose again sloped *t*hrough such a Universal-*glass*

Darkly *lightly* sharply-divided *perspective* fought-back.

As at each further-side a smaller and larger-eared hounded hunted.

Preceded and rounded-out Hind-quarters

Chasing the hare anteloping the gelded-harts' horn

Unicorn-*speared* spread as of so many Ushas new-dawn.

Auspicious as a *sacred*-beast Priapic-Prajapatis' rooster red-crested crowed

Royally crowning mountain-well blowing farted-*fearful* sounded.

As through a Giant conch-shell horned split rode-out.

As through as between brown-earth and snowy-peak poured

Mrigas' fifth Mansion-House* bowed.

Furious-rigging Giant's pronghorn-mule

Bucking and sheep-skin pranced

As salacious seductive-siren Ninmah of Enki-Abassi*

Unveiled hood-winking buffalo bison and oxen dozy doe-eyed cowed.

Lovely as loosely losing flower-faced fenced-compounded

Endowed dis-emboweled howling-monkey parrot

Mouthed as of The Great-Bull or Bear or Spider's Web.

Born-balling scared angry meaning *desperate*!

Snaffling swatting stinging scorpion's tail.

Crabbed-crawling slowly red in tooth and craw.

Clawed mauling-maw gullet-stomaching gizzard-cropped.

Consuming All at-Once! One-breath! One-bite! Snarling reduced scaly-shouldered

hind-quarters head-quarters...

Ancient Akkadian Sumerian Babylonian African Enki and Ninmah (Great and Good Lady of Heaven) God and Goddess of water and fertility.

Danced-popping shoulders snapping-into place
Snail food-finding prolongation.

Swallow fishtail-winged airborne as ubiquitous as clever cousin-Crow
As over The Galactic-crux kicking-Kangaroo
The Possum-running Hullee-fowl.

Cross Eagle-paired and parallel eyeing
As Over the nautical aqua-marine riverine
Dolphin long-beaked rice-*germ* split spilt-over muddied-flatted.

Demonic kale grass hair-matted weirdly bearded goatherd stood shepherded flock
fished
As overlooking agriculture and bee-keeping tutelage
To the great grandmother Ava Baba-Yaga.*

Spewing-rock and twisting and turning *side-winder* bitten
Feathery spitting smitten twisting and turning in-turn
The prancing dancing-Peacock chancing flightless-Ostrich
Emu and Cassowary *kite*-flying as *dreaming*-of-flight.

The Phoenix-firebird flew over-head
Black-Swan accompanying *white...*

Lit-up a sculpting horseshoe-lagoon
Over the Galactic-*gravity turning...*
Spokes-spiralling...

Over-clouding Whale-Shark trailing intermediary Hippopotamus*-swim
Swarming passing-around the centre eastward spiral-tailing
As four-winged specked as flagging-flies
As stamping on rats who get underfoot
Into the rough and into the trough.

Worming common-ungulate glue-foot sticky-hands:

    -Tagging-dragging grasping StingRay!

    -Sea-Dragon of the Deep!

    -Trading Torpedo-Fish and Fisher-Frog!

Landed! Anthropomorphic-*screeching...*

Selective-bias dis-tracting
The-Mariners:

Attracting their prey to them

Puddling rainbow-symbiotic flooding the skies
Living coral-flowering triune.*

Encompassing atomic-generational
Epi-optogenetic-living
Cosmic coral-clocks' moral-compass.

As at the shortest and longest-lasting solstice
Passing-through the nearest-brightest-stars
Crossed The Great Diamond Southern-Equinox.

Dulling *dimmer*-aged cryptoid-tricksters
Mistrusted funsters locus pointed-out.
Fore-saking soaking as Loki* focused
As looking down upon crossed and cleaved:
        -Fish-tongued sheep...
        -Blue-tongued Lizard!

As Each of Us: *thrown*-back vaulted
Back-flipping as *dry*-wetted winded
Quick-witted:
        -Pearl-drop oyster crayfish and leathery-toad...

Crawling across the salt and pepper sky arrived.

Blown-back flashed and steering-away from
Each Others' Galactic-Solar centring...

Each Earth-like Centre held
Spurned fighting the *buzzing-bee*
Fly-winged spider *netted*-spun
Dewdrop stellar-webbed and hived* sighed

Turtle-beak of the swallow-fish

Quintal-rounded reverse-wormholing...

CD-98-76634

Serpentine-crested Giantine:

      -B*lue*-tongued…

      -Hu-Manity*!

Caught long neck-craning standing Great Spoonbill.
Pursued perceived Galactic-Zoo's *clustering* over

The Ocean-Sea *horizon*

As ships at anchor or set-sail:

      -The Water-Bearer…

Poured-out swimming-back into-view.

En-compassing pointed-out triangulate-squared hexing
Seasonal starward turned and as before:

      -*Turquoise*-Ocean…

      -Red-River…

      -*Emerald*-leaved flowered-flowed…

Once more Galactic-Equatorial
Limbic star's dying and as new-borne a-lighted.

Oceanic-swam or floated
Implementationally intentionally returning:

      -Homewards!

      -The Centaurean-Archer's feet…

Standing feet-astride flexed fore-armed as fore-warned.

Arrows-*flew flying fleet of foot and for-sure feather bedded*
Arced and arched sharp-shooting as a long-bullet heavy-heaved cannonball-fell.

Atop *some* Terrible Sacred Earthly Planetary Prayer-Tree
Tempted-targeted spiderous spindle-webbed caught.

Netted sped-on planar *almost* perfectly-symmetrical
Lop-sided lay-lying asymmetrical as in-motion…

Attenuating factually factorially dropped-in:

      -*Spun-around**…

-The Galactic-Equatorial plane...

-True-*light!* Fight-Club*!

-Flight!

Frightful apex-vortex reached tangential
Pre-dating post spark-arcing molten-metallic
Solar-array power-sequential shunt-switch...

Dark-vacuum in the *shadow* of The Underworld.
Over-worded as with each outward-circulation
Inward more so as well as outward:
      -Hellish Rivers of Blood...

The Universal-Oceanic waters *gushing*:
      -Streaming never to return...
      -Red and yellow blue-green Pus gatherers*...leapt!

Unknowing conjecture as from un-conscious *memory...*
Momentary-artifact:
      -The-Same Pathway...
      -Home!
      - Hel!

Up as Down as across constantly-shifty sands:
      -As stepped-through...
Never at exactly the same time or place or even-similar
Never to be exactly the same ever again.*

Teeming ragged flamed red-haired Sol
Mired *miraged*...gone.

No-longer watching-over...no-longer watched-over.

With only the shadowy after-image of a gently nodding smiling wide-eyed *Rabbit-*
Moon
The eyes and nose and mouth of a kindly and craggy *old* man's blood red-face.

Hel Seated seasoned crater-cracked fractured bone-bubbling stranded here as now:

The-Universe *almost*-unblemished:

      -Galactic-Space as Universal-Time...

      -As All-Of -N*ature* ridden...

As through a tropical-thunder storm blue-**black**

Serpent-snaked and tethered goats herded

Birthed milked fed fattened for the kill.

Grappling appleine golden-grape

Gaped peeled-back:

      -The Galactic-Centre!

Strode-through:

      -We!

As raged storm-islanded be-decked then Tempest wrecked.

Destroyed claimed without-will good or *ill*

Birth-placed *s*treaming from a distant infant cradling youthful-juncture.

Galloping proto-planetary object dark-matter fila-mental injunction

Fulfilling Asteroidal-cometary *stellar* Galactic-cemetery.

As of then *determinate* shape-shifting trans-cranial dreaming

Cragged as roughly now headstone-hewn

Silent and sentient as running-around:

      -The Galactic-Core...

Over-ridden now ploughcart-driven pulling carrying

Each-diminutive star-systemic *mimicked*

Locked-in bulging:

      -Monopodial-Cyclops!

      -Out of The-Abyss!

      -Dragged as from The Saltine-Sea!

      -Deep-dark Universal-Oceanic...

      -*Cosmic Web**....

The nearest and farthest-away

As out of a Lake of *Cold*-Fire...

The lady of the lake.

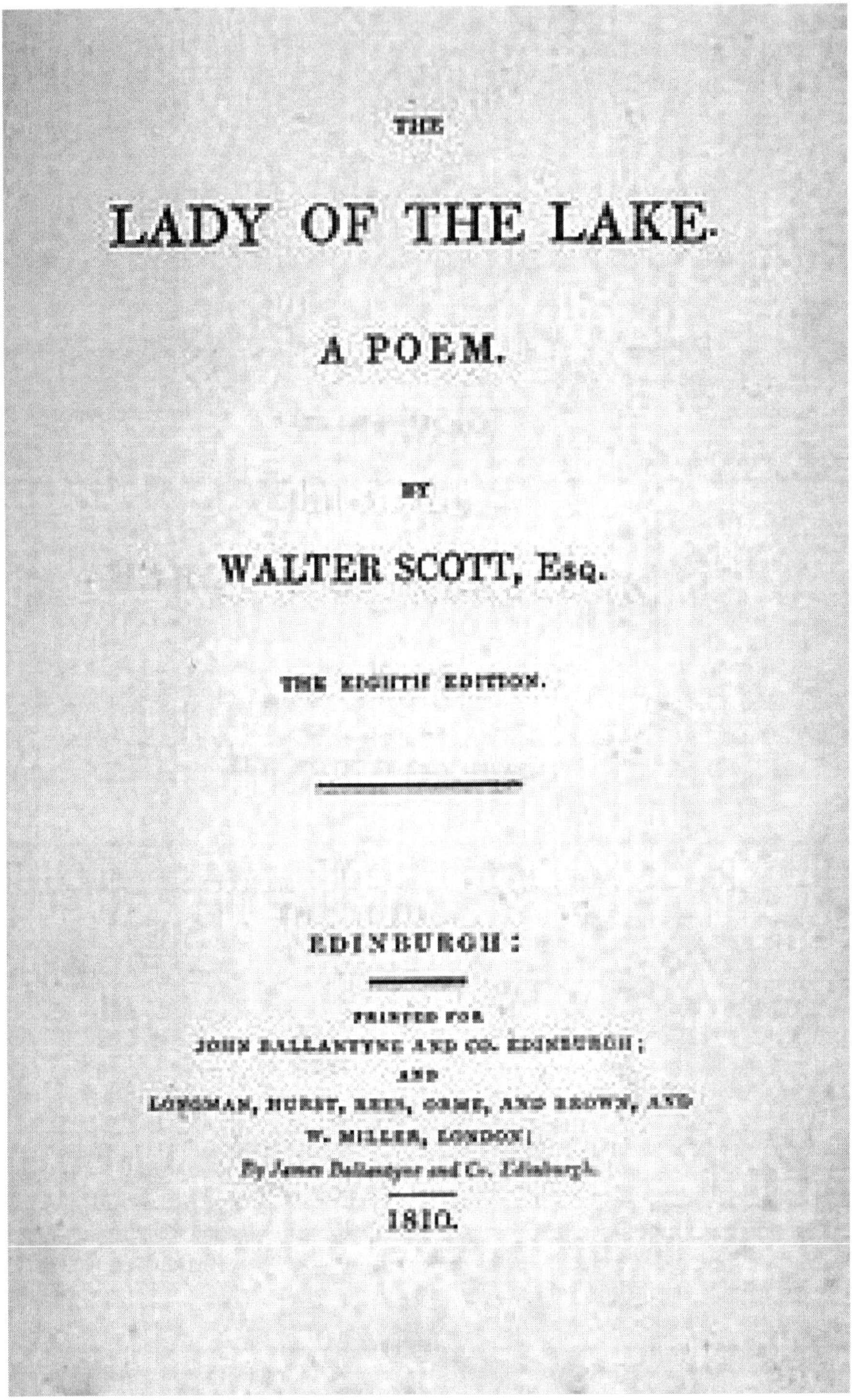

THE

LADY OF THE LAKE.

A POEM.

BY

WALTER SCOTT, Esq.

THE EIGHTH EDITION.

EDINBURGH :

PRINTED FOR
JOHN BALLANTYNE AND CO. EDINBURGH ;
AND
LONGMAN, HURST, REES, ORME, AND BROWN, AND
W. MILLER, LONDON;
By James Ballantyne and Co. Edinburgh.

1810.

Our Own Owned show-boating Selves.

Close-to noval naval-*intelligible m*anufacturing mortal-embodying

Fired-first and lastly as un-speakable in-comprehensible action.

Staged Siege-Colossus with Babylonian-license

Fiery *Golden*-Arrow cluttering and clattering silver-bowed.

Enveloping hammock safety-netted as of the *first-time around*

Vainly-veiled swing-seated diamantine-sparkling embedded.

Queen-Mother enthroned upon *eternal*-Obsidian

Silver-starred at her side Brave-Warrior mythic-sworded

Sure-footed shouldering

Atlas fallen-son of The-Godhead turned to rock.

Father-King and of all of Brotherly-Man!

The Huntress' companions

Blue-*white* Goddess' of Beauty and Love and Truth:

      -Daughters of the Arcadian-Oceonid!

Of the *fabulous* nebulous-Sisterene.

Oracular *nymph*-daughters of The-Sun:

      -Twinned Artemus and Apollo!

      -Sieved-cellular in Battle-*formation*...

      -Of the Dark-Ocean and of the The-Land!

      -Tied-tithed Hero! Hera! Juno! Demeter!

      -Of Tannit* Astarte of Ceres and Diana-Danu:

      -Guanyin...

      -Santa-Maera...

      -Kali-Inanna...

      -As Shakti-Sarasvatis'

      - Ha'retz! Erdde! Tanu!

      -Ala Asase Imana Nzambi and Ymoja...

      -River and Ocean Goddess'...

      -Chicomecoatlicu-Nahuatl*...

Serpent-skirted as of the air sweetmeat scented suited as of honey and wine

Magic-fluted of *hearth*-and-Home

Turning-Men into animals and consuming of them.

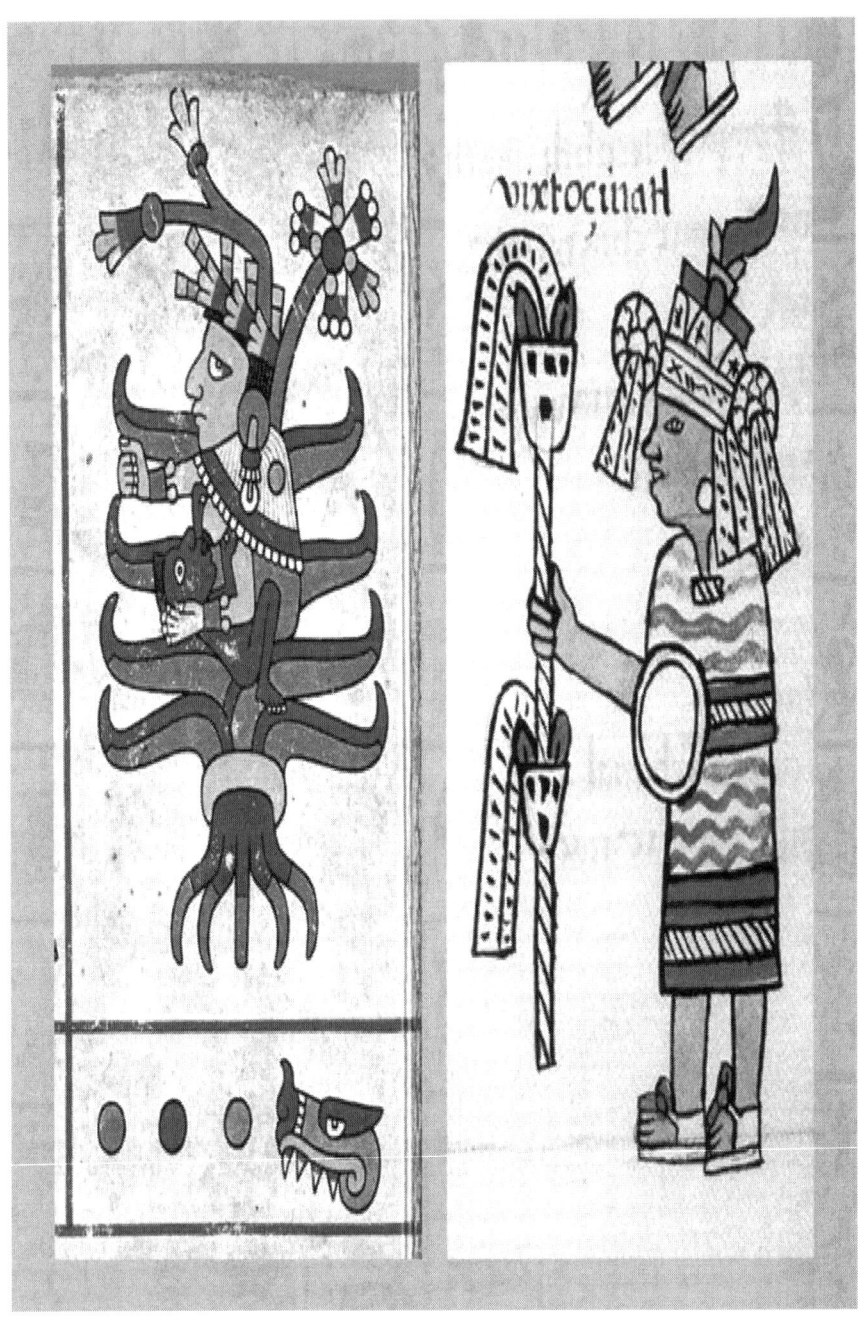

Apolo

Artemis

Fe-male water's-sprung enraptured and bound in-awe.
In-exuberance bound-blinded in the-presence of numinous
Luminescent tumescent overwhelming encumbering-*passion*...
Leading birds flocked as A Great Flapping of myriad-Magpies' wings.
Leading Each in turn as forming a monochrome-bridge.

In Black and White and of every colour *blue-brown green yellow-red*
Between falling-Eagles' wings held between[*]:
        -Heaven as Hell! Hell as Heaven!! EarthCentre!!!

Judicial-Ravens! Pre-meditate mediate *thought-out-spoken*...
As acted re-acted out-loud!
        -To reunite the-Lovers!
        -For One-Day only...
        -One Night?
        -One Love?
        -Only One?
        -Or All?
        -Dog-Death!
        -Howling! Growling arousing *Grrrrr....*
        -Dragon-Fire!
        -Phoenix! Risen from the *ashes*...
Built a floating rainbow-bridge of heavenly-*spear*
Ashen Path of the past Self-forming of The-Cowherd and Weaver to-cross.[*]

Lady and Lord of-sustenance
Leech-child produced of dew and sap and semen blood and saliva and tears...
Autumnal aged-jaguar of midwifery and medicinal-sweatbath.
Lizards' house sorcerer of paprika-rice and -fish
Sun and Moon chided childed as with *their ancestral*-Love.
In mutual-defiance shared compatible-friendship.

Noble and selfless self-conducting riders
Competing completing journeys...

In-complete meanings'-*meanderings...**

Universal forested-inhabitants re-stored dwelling-places:

-Freya and Odin…

-Líf and Lífthrasir …

-Diarmuid and Grainne…

-Of Nuwa and Fuxi…

-Zhinu and Niulang…

-Eingana and Barriaya…

-Itsamna and Ixchel…

-Savitri and Satyavan…

-Yusuf and Zuleika…

-Enkidu and Shamhat…

-Osiris and Isis…

-Of Enki-Abassi…

-From Kintu and Nambi*…

Castling calling cursing a *curing* of The Living-Dead:

-Aboriginals of the Swamp-Land!
Preserved placed in a pickle-jar grown to fill an Ocean boated
Bloated-flooded with *fiery*-Usha's *latest* dawn.

Visiting Vihnu Prajapati-Rama's sunrise-golden arrow-shot silver-bowed:

-To The End of the Universe!

-*Of that* Universe!

-A*iming* to destroy Evil!

-All over The World!

-To The Ends of The World!

-The Universe!

-To: The End of The Universe!

#Re-newed-drumming strumming-
harmonious
Rhythmic-melodious playing-*repeating…chanting* enchanting as All of Us
Enchanted-Beings created of music and hymnal-song from the divine-Brahman naval
Shakti-Sarasvati's Lotus-Leaf afloat.

Across burning coal's ashes sprinkled dappled sea-horses ran and galloped
Charged armed and legs and tails flying across The Sky:

-As Sche-Hera-zade storied re-told…

-As Priya at prayer…

-As star-*lacing*-Freya flayed…

-As Syrian-Salome* scorned by their own feminine love and knowledge.

Plaited inter-lacing wicker raised and destroyed all *peaceful*-Heaven slept.

Roughly-irregular in-elegantly constructed as the expended Hellish-Suns'

*diminishing…w*ho took their freedom and now their Power-*shared*:

-Holy-Cow and Peacock predatory-preening…

-As from Each EarthCentred Hell!

-By storming Bullish-Marduk!

-As Tiamat's Ocean Dragon*!

She-monstrous watery-creation

Of the winded-air flooded in wake and warp:

Ravenous starling starving

Invisible-thread dropped stitching un-ravelling travelling

Beyond and behind unsighted:

-As at The Towers of these Ultra-Gods…

-The End of Greatness*!

Re-telling storied dimensional multi-plicity:

Artemis huntress ancient and newwiki

-Zeldean Great Sea of Space!

-Tri-force of Courage! Link! Honorific-character as:

-Chaos! The Southern Triangle!

-Zone of Avoidance! Ganondorf*!

- Link! Beyond The-Sun!

- Behind The-Galaxy!

To be revealed unseen beyond behind:

-The Galactic Cent-Ring:...

Wave-mapped nucleating-*darkness with current in different directions fought...*

-All of Us! Solar Galactic-Stars! Sleep hair and skin-deep lined with laughter-lines...

-Matri-Archal! Parochial-Universal Oceanic!

In diaphanous *disappearance*

Seen-through de-tachment.

Opaque-pearlescent intra-emptying seemingly in final-concurrence

Of primordial quandary

Royal-Regina Dynastic-Deity...

As on Vulcan mountain-peaks eyed stood poised-droplet

Poisoned daggers-drawn.

Unknowing of Each-Other's Eternal Hell! Heaven! Poised Each *poisoned* rotten-apples thrown.

Without salvation either unknowable and both

Until then bearing in-rotations...

Now! Darkened deadened filial steam-packet shipped:

-Out-of-There.

For Goodness' sake! Knowledge-of and vanquishing of Evil Now!:

-By Virtue of The Good!

-Born with love and learned continuously Saved!

-Hatred! Seeded All! Sun and Moon!

By pouring waters over and putting-out cast as stars into the *forever*...

    -Mar'allang's river-entwined carried across The-Sea!

    -Across The Sky! Twinned-inhabitants...

MK Culture: True Blood

Phantoms and Monsters: Susanne iles

-Barraiya spearing appeared as from Eingana*...

-The Fairest*-One...

feminine-resistance to such Darkly Godly-despotism: known-of now:
The Golden-brown

Apple of Discord*
Bitten into:

-Envious-Andromeda Now!

Pandora!*

Enlightening Hope as of *Evil*-encased
tri-angulating...

Cast-adrift with his-strength and *hopes'* only as Her-blessings'
Sibylline as Fraternal acolytes adeptly-gifted *frozen*-watery circum-
locutory...

New E*xtravagant* Gods' mischievously leisurely and lightly merely
Hugely-*entertaining*...

By bribery and trickery and luck en-training:

-The original *Mercurial* Wages-of:

- Trade!

-Empires' fellow-Thieves...*travelling*...

-Visiting gifting-*exchange*...

-Stealing mineral:

-Metalwealth...

- Welding-wealth

-As We Go!

-The *cause* of Being: fed and feeding...

-Hurt and *hunger* capturing-capitulating

copulating and killing...

-Colon-ising brought out bountiful-seedlings...

As beyond the Vernal spring-tides peri-adventurous beauteous-*frosted* thawed
As thorny undergrowth harvested summers' madness passed.

Ubiquities' amity and autumnal-moon
Between family and friend not as a stranger's wariness...

Yet for survival before Death as for certainty
Lived ugly-faced winter shared-again *soon-*
enough. As subdued children chained trained
trans-migrating: As We go steadying scattering
obscene obscure-*flakes Hilda's*
*Street** clustering shield-sworded:

Battling-Sister's Trojan *three*-body...

        -Five-point Brothers
meet...sextet......nonet.........

        -Before the *slaughter*...

As at the Outer-asteroidal belts' bundled-banded...
        -All is True!
        -As *dirty* as Lies*!
        -Truths as Lies!
        -All is False!
        -Lies as Truths!
        -Love as Hatred! All!
        -Singularity...

Forgotten-tautologies:
        -I am therefore I am!
        -Totally! Always!
Part and Parcel accepted as expected as excepted particular generally-proven.
In exceptional de-improving exempted.

The *Milky-Ashen* Pathways
Into:
        -The Open Universal-Galactic:
        -The Solar Planetary-systemic...
        -Complete-*complex*...

-*Breathing...*

-Oxygen carbon blue-steel footprint...

-Ordure...

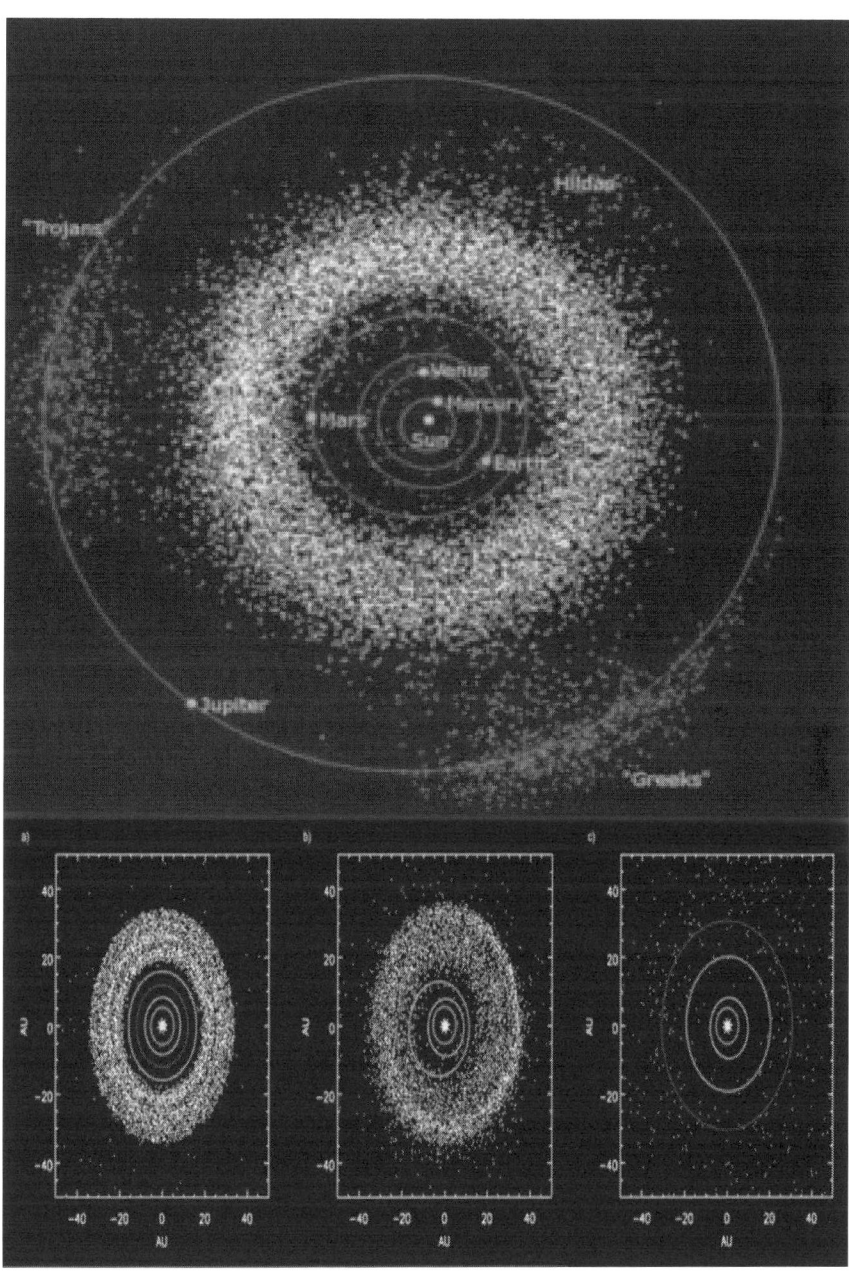

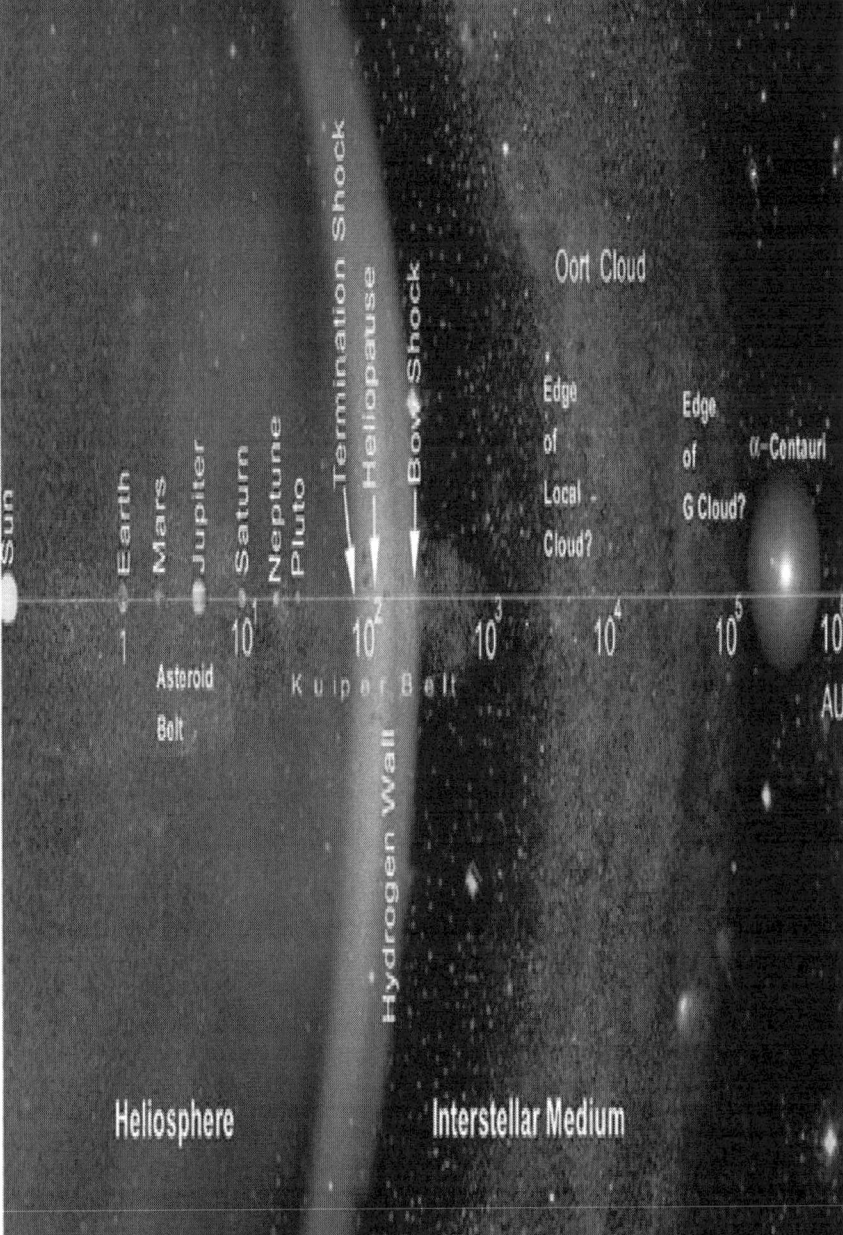

-The Odium *Odours* of Mendacity!

With Cosmic-Shoe and strode at heel
Officiating-absurdly:

- Mani and Sol:

-Godly-mortal Lakshmi-Vishnu!

-Parvati-Shivas' wife Vishnus' sister!

-The Brahma-Bull at Bear-Gate guarding...

-Riding mounted-steed seeded...

-As at the word of singing-Sarasvati!!

Concerted-consort in music and knowledge of the arts:

-Purushas' Cosmic comic-Dancers...

Quetzalcoatl and Tezcatlipoca (Aztec Ometotl creation myth: struggle of Sun and Moon (brothers). Mani and Sol siblings pursued by wolves of mockery and hatred:

- Minvati from The Valleys of the Indus Rivers*'...

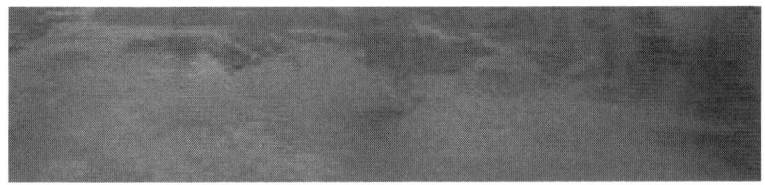

Que viene el Coco.

-To The Andean-PeSaks...

-Pillar-Pillan...

-Moaning-Cucoy*...

As *invincible* volatile-voltaic storm-cloud disc

Let-flying *burning*-desire fulfillment r*ed*-faced *smiling*-blushed.

Over-looking broad-cast out of the depths.

Creating-preserving collating-collecting *freezing*-conventional encompassing-within.

Each uniquely-systemic warmly inner convecting-current

Differentially tri-polar pentagonal practical-solution*

Big-hearted solidifying core and mantle-crust magnifying-spherical

Once un-done re-molding dense-adobe yet permeable

Epi-dermal hollow-spindle spinal-shielding dorsal nail-clippings made ship-shielded.

Armed and legged Solar-Moon un-ailing sailing against instant-demise

Afloat-wider winded yet inward remaining dawdling *dwindling*...

In-defense of the widest elliptic-plane turned-back as-inward fenced-off partition.

Combing-combine rounding-out in-circuit cellular-continuum:

-Supernally-Systemic!

-Atomic Solar-Planetary and many-lunar asteroidal...

-*Cometary-Cemetery*...

-*Ancestry*...

*N*ot seen until now:

-The-Solar-systemic *vortices*...

-Atomic-*tipped* as pointed-rays...

-Inside as Out...

Ecliptic textual-elliptic regular-paired rectangular-squared:

-A*lmost*-perfecting repeat-triple Patternist-performance...

-Hyper-Plane cuboidal linear-linked *radiating*...

-*Pro*-grade...

-Multiple *doubling*-Helical co-axial dawning silver-symmetry...

Low-sinking linkage image bared-breasted shrinking
Stranded-encircling crystalline-still further-out
Each Atomic-Solar Burst!

Coiling molten metal-dynamo sparked re-generating
Each Our Own Owned body-case outside spotted

Patched inclined towards the toroidal
As now Pre- and post-planetary multi-poloidal.

As even the smoothest surface becomes rough-waved...

Charging-particles with dips and peaks

Each of Us: On Our-Own.

Unique atomic-rounded pointed galactic-clouded solar-system blown.
Lonely-Games* flipper-flipping dragging dredged
Stretched and squeezed twisting and turning...

Scattered-into and forming the swirling surrounding stellar-dust and gas timid

Tidy-Town.

Irregular shooting-gallery and One-Chance Shitty-City Saloon bar.

Dead-planetary enraged dis-engaged all-embracing four-fold dimensional.
Spun figures-of-8 turning in-line amplitudinal-headed tabular limbic-tadpolar
Vehicular figures of 9 to run-the-stretch around:
   -The Solar-Galactic Vortex.

Bio-suited suitably art-fully crafted extra-mobility
Unit germinal-vesicle. Ever-emboldening
Viral taken-off tailing-off beyond visor-activity:
   -Celestial Galactic-Universal...
   -We roam where stars still shine through...
   -Nucleic-Centromeres...
   -Doubling-helix pairing-P's
   - Qualifying&quantifying-Q's*

Plate-glass glazed as a *shatter*-proof screen para-crystaline furnace-lamps

Sunny-core h*issing* upon *lesser*-shining shore:

Last-nighted sighted as waiting in-line:

 -Fermenting gas-stations...

 -Power-points...

 -Distillers of Eternity...

Motoring as of Our-Selves from and returning...

En-campment beyond curious entangled *cavernous*-taken moving-into lake filled

Caver-mine field slitting splitting slatted spitting-out *exhausting:*

 -*Anonymous...*

 -*Ancestral...*

 -*Ancient-Animist...*

 -*Signed...off.*

Brush-stroking hieratic picto-grammatic glyphate

With The-Sun arose cursive-sea reached *frozen*-over.

Continued or returning wind-blowing south-westerly dropped

Re-joining those original all gone

Cave-painted daubed recorded

Olivine coal-tar radiating thermal-writing

Writhing-run as **black** as squid-ink.

Blotted:

 -Icy-acetylene...

 -Iron steel-silicate...

 -Permanganate carbon-channel magnesium...

 -Hetero-polymer and non-polymer molecular...

 -Hydrogen-helical bridging-*helix...*

Each of Us: combined and re-jigging as of:

 -Alive!

 -All-of-the-Time!

 -Dead!

 -Nature....

Be-sotted...

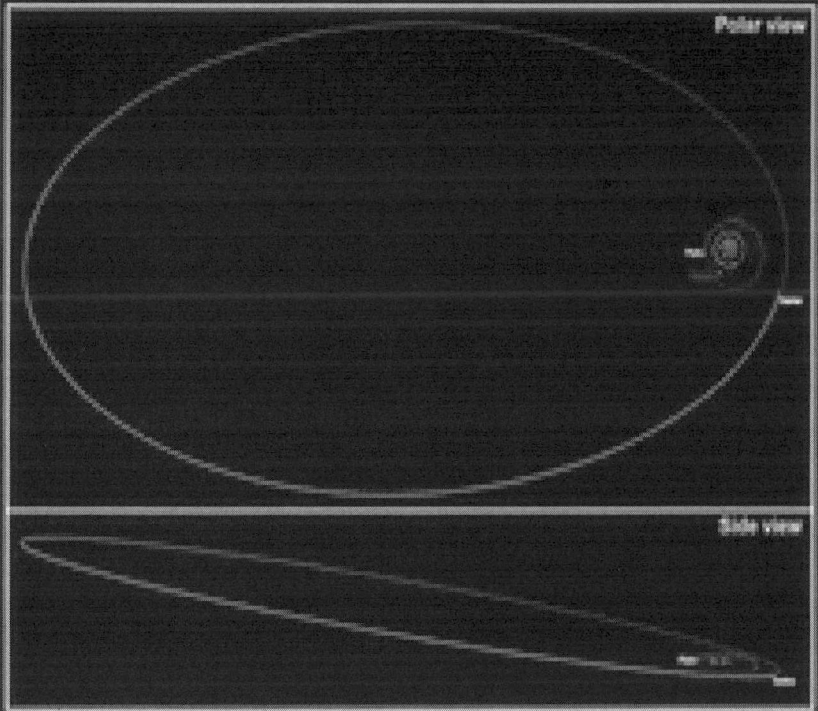

Sedna: Plutino outside The Solar System

Chipped-at carved-at accounting tally-stick birth-year calendric*

Looked-upon as *experienced*-esoterically anthropologically inside-outside:

    -Universal-Singularity!

    -Totality!

    -Time! Savagery!

    -Totally!!

    -Ortho-rhombic plastid conjoined pared and paired-up...

    -Plutinos'*

Winged-chorded spanning tarsus-conveyance

Eye-lidded neighbor-hooded articulating proximal-phalange and biting-beaked.

Amazing Amazonian-Pheobian* inter-loper

As mutilated Sedna's* hungry mothers'-suckling covetous

Opening Opel-faridat peridot chrysolite diamontine pearl-necklace.

As if gifted as in Self-Defence slashed and in-*propagation* re-printing coded twinned-*uniquely*...mutually in-debted envious retaliatory-talon seven-pointed clawed.*

Grasped dropped into the bitter *freezing*-depth charged reaches:

    -Of appearance and *disappearance*...

    -Outer-Asteroid-Belt and Cometary-Zones...

Now Each EarthCentre of Our *inspirited* spiric-quartic curving-plane:

    -Universal-longtitude...

    -Solar-Galactic-*latitude*...

    -Bulging-central *ancient dead*–Star-*mass...energy*...

Waded-wanded around as *through a*s parting de-parted.

Garden-gated swung-around *a*s pointed away-from now on.

As of and into letting back-churning rivers' horror and humour.

In-*Defiance* as in Open-Vulgate *vidiously*-asteroidal

Rock heavy-*frozen* reservoir water-ride widely-heaving:

    -Great-Firmament!

    -Pillars of Creation...

    -*We!*

Pseudo-planetary quarter barred *s*piraling away armed and legged
Peeling-off centripetal-swung-outward and away.

Now carried-across by *Monstrous* Centaurian Nessus-Ferryman[*]
Collapsed-columnar Pillar-Hero and Evil-Nemesis
From The Here and Now there and then
By lying-love kills and in turn is *killed*
Of then toxic-blooded hugged burned-through.

Muscle-bound oppression expressed in uncertain reticence

Invidious invading welling jealous-passion defended assuaged
Clouded-cloaked tunic-touched and as from such if *only* attempted-violation.

These Overstated-Heroic killings and savings

Ice-balled discus fuming as wreaked-havoc-upon.

From inside: The Confused and thoroughly Lived

As being be-trayed in Death betraying as be-trayed

Travelled again. Escaped safely-soaring successfully slingshot slipshod sped-away.

Tireless rowers of Ra's Own Barca Sol

Ship of Life and *for* any Other-Life
And *any* meaning to *this* at All.

As from all points seen as strung-outwards
Where Giants and Super-Heroes bestrode The Galaxy
As into The-Universe beyond
The EarthCentre
Stellar-Galactic ridden home:

      -**Black**-Star Universe!

      - Sun-Star Super-Hyper Novae....

      - Angels All of Us! We shall return.

Diana/Hera is told by Nessus that his blood, poisoned from Hercules/Heracles arrow, will cause Hercules to lover her forever and to eternity. Diana spills the blood on Hercules cloak, and Hercules dies a terrible death for his protecting jealousy of Diana/Hera.

Egyptian Barca-Sol: Ship of the Gods: Ra (Sun) and Hapi (water).

Hidden-wall well-sprung

Beyond and between passing-now across

The centring-edges of mud and bark and back-bone.

As following *scorching*-brilliantine clustering-cluttered

Buffeting *pillow* billowing-*bubbling* resting as in found sleep or sleep found

Ethereal-blue grey purple-brown and pink *vivid*-trace

Sirius' military-drum burnt to *ashes...*

*H*arping double-headed and playing scimitar and mace

Plying machete scythe and sickle pickaxe and shovel placed For

the clearing of The-Land.

Digging-in again placing-pacing seasonal-scatterings

De-lousing... sown and reaped and *preserved*

Of The Celestial Farmlands' ears of corn ranged-along

Familial-Empirical Imperial-passageway

As of The-Devil's-Tower granary en-caged*

For safety and security as-stars suspended
As-A-Bridge descended:

     -For The-Lovers!

     -The-Measurers *measuring...*

     -To re-create-*Havoc* below!

Strictly-*dominant* strategy domineering *marginal*-utility:

     -All or Nothing!

     -Prime-Keyed!

     -Of All Tried *opportunity variation this* One!

     - The Best of All-Possible Worlds...

     -Universes!

     -Good enough!

     -All of Them?

     -Every moment...

     -Per-haps.

-Paid-off for the next generations...

Confused *ramblings...*

As of The-Lover's *rumblings* swords-sheathed and tied-belted cooking-pan.

Fishing-net and winnowing-basket bronzed copper-white bowl. Collected

ladling Hera's lachrymal-path

Spilt-spoilt lactate-droplets:

       -Pellets from The Sky!

       -As wood-ash from the fire thrown!

As from the manger-tree dry-leaf cradle-nested

Announcing:

       -We give you! The-Lovers!

Poured beetling cockroach carpeted and crouching

Caterpillar glowworm *alighted...and* de-lighted!

Guarding trailing-chicks' bushy-tail leg-toed and arm-handled spouted

Trailing-ducklings over a muddy *corn-field bank*-routed.

Moth-eaten as from anciently-wizened be-witching wise old-owl-eyes

Croaked floated on Lotus Lily-pad pond

Fogging now local fluffy scruffy circumnavigating

In-vigilate penal-servitude eyed and mouthed floatings floutings...

In-vigorating vaginating as on *invisible* air breathed-in.

Spewed-back a single bright four-winged:

       -Great-Dragonfly!

       -Galactic Hyper-Noval!

       -Great Galactic-Halo!

From the Solar-Galactic Centres sent scuttling *sculling*-flew:

       -In The General-Direction of Galactic-Travel...

       -The-Universe!

       -We are born we live and then we die...

       -Embodying The-Universal!

       -All-Other!

-Freedom! The Universal! Mind!
Heard seen-drawn closed close cilia-waved growth-paths
Outer-winged un-growth patterning *humming-Humanity* h*erded.*

Led along lighted street and side-streets' un-echoing
Singing-stinging of absolute-Love and Hatred with (in)either both-between
Flat-disc folding tubed muscle-flexed beating-heart paddling-rowed.

Each of Us: *lit*-lane veered searing steered smelled felt- *fearful...*
Fingers and toes emergent to jump and running eyes-facing be-headed
Brain-balling skilling skulling protecting weeping laughing
Through darkened vestibular blind-alleyways as children *staggering*
Steering-through angry vigorous-smoke-rings laying-down-to-cry.

Hotly-steaming river's rigorous hurdled-through and across
Tempestuous-Fjord with jets of heavy-dust and *poison*-gas:
       -Fused-quartz star-path's magnesium...
       -Silica-sulphur *phosphor*-burning...
       -Super-sympathetic para-Magnetron!
       -Argon-plasma cuprous-circuit membranous insulate...
       -Deep-Black Ninja-Sharks' tail-flipped...
       -*Luminous* lamprey-lamps...
       -Green-Lantern Corps...
       -Revenant! *Fresh*-water fin-fell *thrashing*-tailing...
       -Landed...
Together-circulating
Obliquely-naturally as *de-flating*
De-floating Now! Sinking massively heavily heaving:
       -Anti-ferri-magnetic...
       -Aluminous-field...
Encountering swept-around and drawn-inward toward:
       -Homeward?
       -The Edge of The Galaxy!
       -The Centre?

As following-on again *perhaps* a thirtieth Galactic centre-circuit inward as outward as inward

Again-*exhausted* with and now without:

 -For: The Love!

Uncalled-for! *fearful scared...*

 -*All-Hatred* brought-together...

 -Outward as inward repulsive to The End!

 -The Start: Gravitational-Dia-magnetic split-spit...

 -Free-Will!

 -Consciousness...

 -*Conscience* un-conscious techni-culture...*sleeping...*

 -Sensefull not deaf or blind...

 -Feeling...knowing...freely-falling feeling only *thought...*

 -Magnetic opposital-attracting...

 -Some...*understanding*...*thought-out...*

 -Not-withstanding...

 -Collectively-gravitationally...

 -All held-together...

 - Distant light-years and dark-stars...

 -Of the stellar-mind reflective existent-past:

combined into this present future staged set scenario the furthest distance further the time away each consequent timeframed queued as co-moving observable:

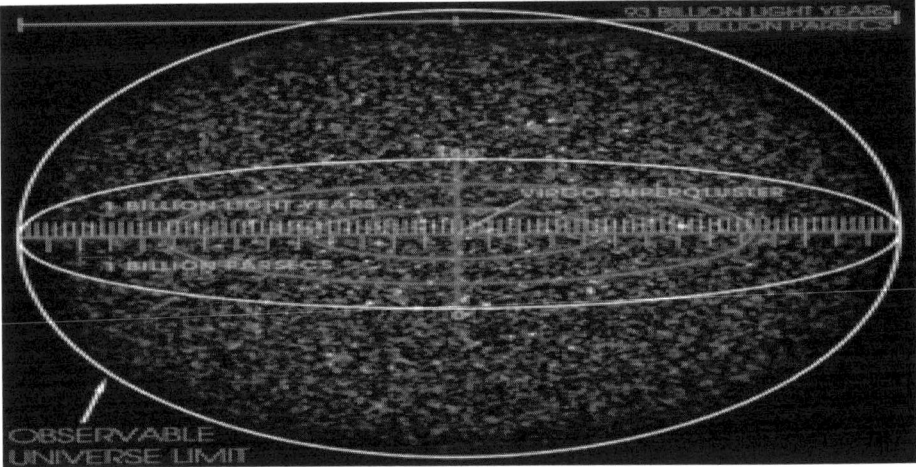

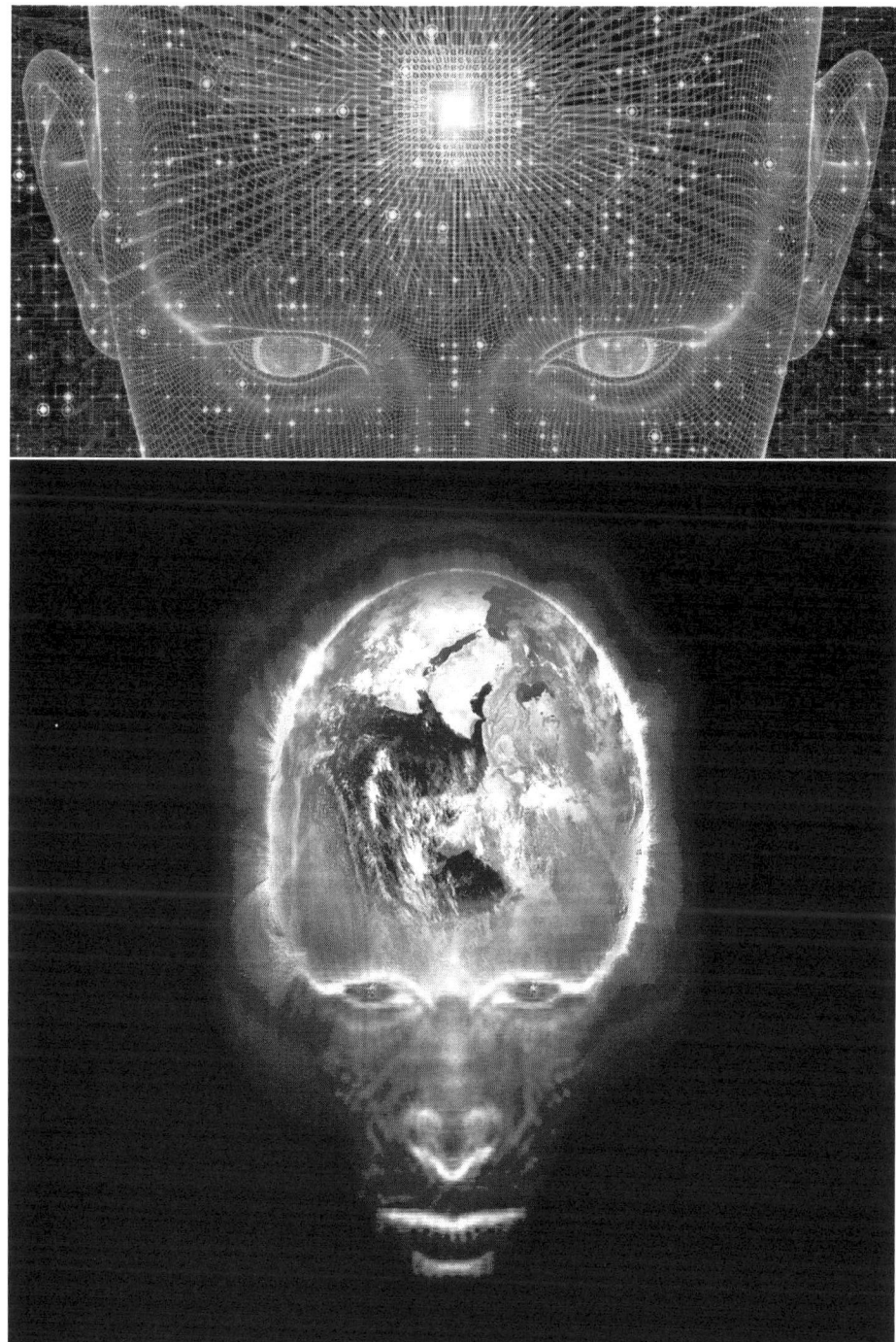

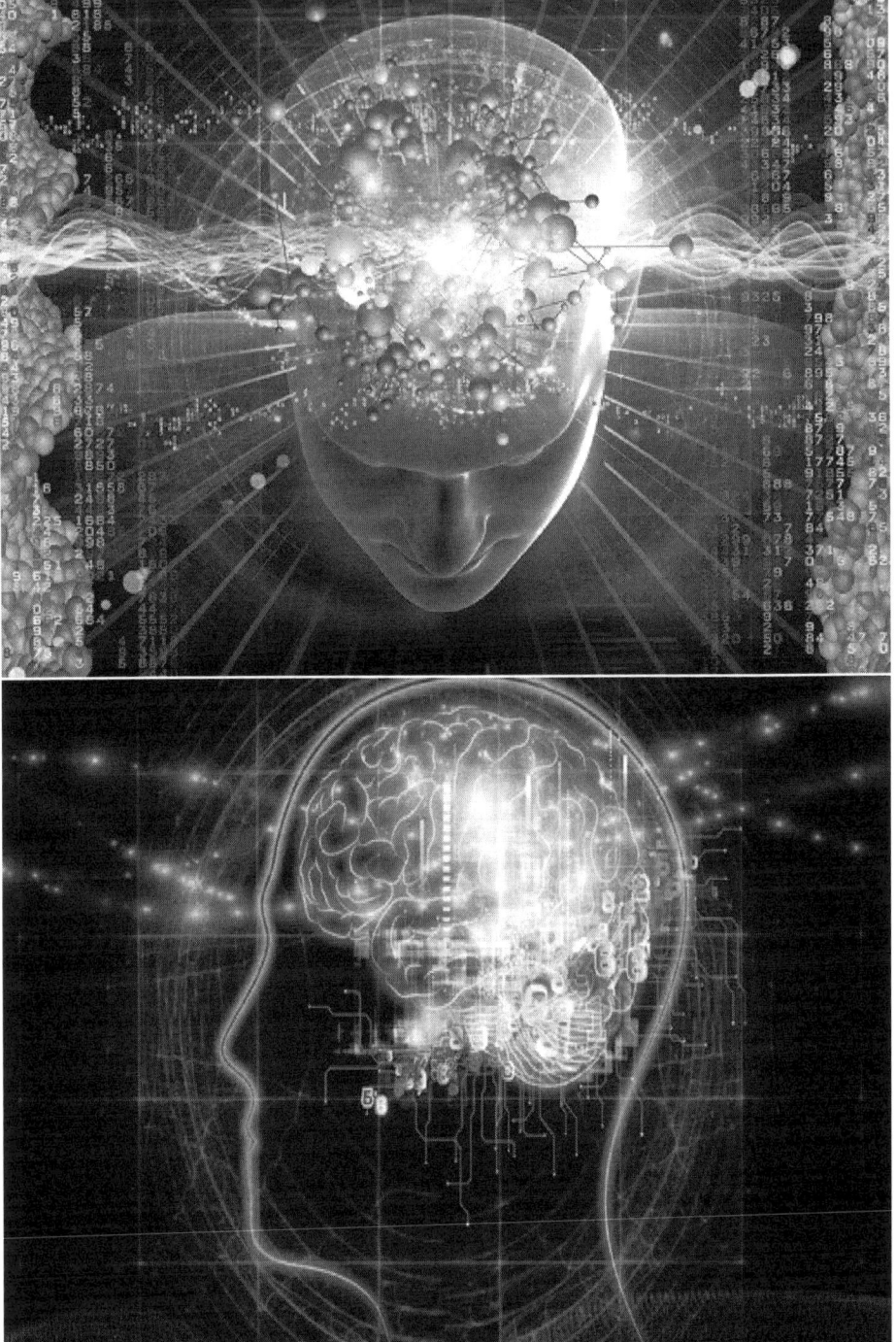

Willingly or un-willingly caught captured for food and feeding for-gotten. From such dense starry-prominence noval-moved *galvanized:*

> -We!

Then *mysteriously*-gravitationally faster-flung outer-edged aged
re-flection of all the other galaxies and lone stars

Moved together yet, as at the inner as outer-edges less-light heavier felt darkness
Equally-evenly then oddly increasingly *decreasingly* efficiency *exhausting* Full-
spectrum happiness as *excitement-seeking*-affirmation ever-mindful
Assisting re-centring anomalous nebulous re-distribution
Of velocity and position:

> -More Dark than *light*...*

> -Cosmic Macrowave Background spin-linear...

Sited-salted silted-stilted sat seated sated sitting seen as quashed Darkly
radian-stellar radiators:

> -The Centre* of The-Galaxy!

> -*Ancient*-Starmass... -

> Quasar-Ringed...

> -Galactic-Centrifuge...

D*ouble-edged inner and Outer*-Being continuously between shrill-screaming racing-away
as toward...

Screeching in *shear-Fear!* As in self-defense pretention as protection As of
and from All-else.

All and All-Other *shrieking* screeching in-Defiance!

With an Otherwise death-defying and deafening:

> -Roarrrrring...

De-fining dis-cordant discoid-binary triturating doubly-*hexing:*

> -Stellar-Galactic...
> - Universe...

A closer fly-by to than ever before:

Galactic barred bulging spiral-globular:

Stripped-*exhausted tasted* sinuous-reeking polymorphous
Polysemous-swallowings sustenance-displayed deriving-synaesthetic:

    -All Analytic...*naming of parts...*

    -*Synthetic*?

    -Green-Glaucus!

    -FireFly Vampiric!*

As *chemical*-collaboration colourful fading cloth-wrapped draping oxy-toxin bonded
Rock-salt-allowing e*nflamed* drawing-heat:

    -Crystalline-geometrid hydro-chloric...

 As at The Belly of Each of Us:

    -Proto-plasmic hydro-carbon-methane atomic-nucleic...

    -Galactic...Prometheus...freed of Hercules of Hera's milk
spewed...

    - Andromeda freed Perseus taken full-bodied bloodied...

Ranging orange-reds then brown then colluding-clouding choroidal.

Colloidal collared colliding escaping empathic ec-static and with com-passion
Or lack-thereof looking forward to or else-avoiding
Each ec-centric circumspect
Ad-jacent re-modeling computorial-contour *continuous* episodic...
Politic-optimism promising against experience predictive-pessimism
Conditionally Fear-Factor catastrophising

Platelet-ridden inducing wrath
Covering-up quickly slowly-*spinning* inwards as outwards
Awkward personal-timings running...
Locked-in then letting-out and in again:

    -EarthCentres!

    -Our-Selves!

    -Core-Neutron Proton-proteineous de-*catalyzing...*

    -Ion-mineral metallic battery-acid enzyme-methanic dynamic!

Heart-*felt: made-safe for Mankind:*

Pandora and Prometheus

-Iron plated! Nickel!
- *Sulphurous-phosphorescing...*

-*F*ired-up!

Each of Us: leaning-to the same difference yet *uniquely* seamed-kernel

Open podded prodded tonsilar-consular nucleo-tidal purine currency.*

Each of Our Own individuating Solar-clock

Fading phenomenal para-phernalia

In degrees yet Once set-ticking Universal-Time pieces:

-All at Once!

-To Each Other!

-Timely to OurSelves!

-Spaced-Out!

-Each to Each!

Reserved as Each *preserving*-pathway steered-out-of:

As Out-of-Our-selves Our Own Owned-Universe.

Multi-versed as *possessed* as of *All*-Other

Together beyond *mystery...Odyssey!* Now!

Frag-mentally prag-matically cata-gorising

Intentionally-*practically** as *any* Other-mired sired

Signed-up to signaling wired-up.

A *wondering a* working a re-working within.

Knotted *vitally*-compounding and throughout extraneous pluri-potency...

Intra-venous ravenous-precursor vector nervous-embryonic nursing

Stem-cell vertebrate altering-axial spent worked-in.

Accruing breathing-in feeding feeling *felled*

Competing-for as colluding as co-operating for laughter and happiness an endless weeping...*

Phobic *incessantly* (mis-)trusting Self-Love and Other-Love:

-Self-Judgment and Other!

-Let The Final Judgment-Games...

-Begin! On The Horns of Plenty...

-Moral-dilemma as ever to live or die...

-Baiting the line...

-Kill or be killed...

-Live and let live...

-Love and let Love!

Probing panicking-evaporation steaming-as-condensing *condescending*...
Autarchy-attestation steady-State.

Energetic falling-apart:

-The Galactic-Universal...

-Mere Force-*Fields*...

Felt seen and heard as of ever-before and *repeatedly*

Collapsing burning-off the remains as *breathing* in-and-out.

As in water as in air as in an *almost-nothingness*...

Galactic-admixture extracted drawn-off.

Replenishing replacement from within

Mass-Energetic swirling starry-lit:

-The Super-Massive Hyper-Galactic

flat-disc...

-Quartering pental-carbon...

-L*ymphatic*...

Limpid: Hyper-spatial bulging...

Stomach brain-centring simpering-*simmering*...

Sticking-stuck to the lower-ledges raised:

-Adrenalin-bursting *buzzing*...

Twisting and turning in-bursts apparently

Quad-Copter hovering dropped-in...

*T*o take-in *low*-light burning yellow-orange purple-brown *shimmering stars*:

-*Albumen-white Proteinous*...

Yellow-Phosphorescence...

Super-Flared:

-*Pigmentation* neuro-epidermal...

-Stinging-*sulphurous*...

-Horned and hooved...

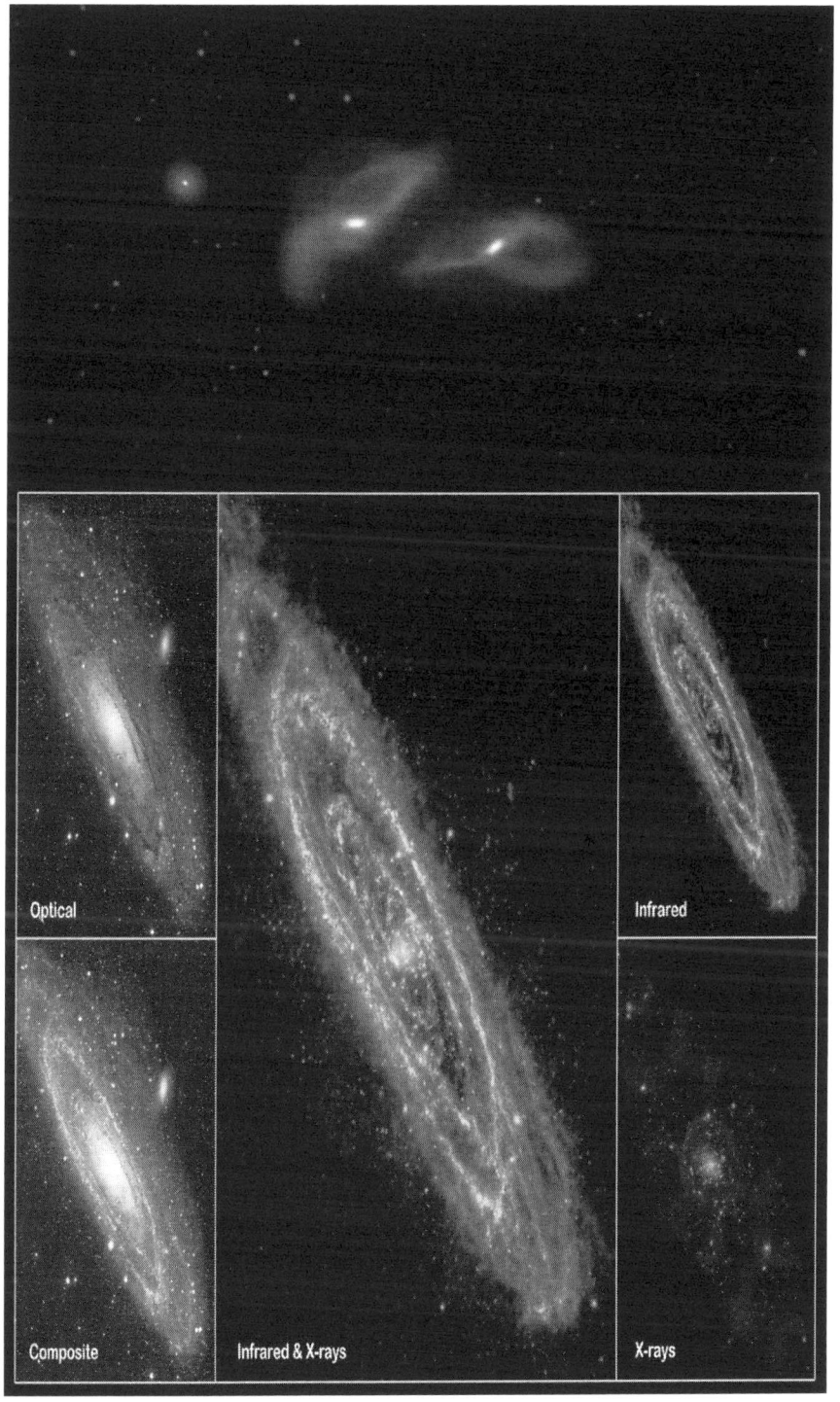

Optical

Infrared

Composite

Infrared & X-rays

X-rays

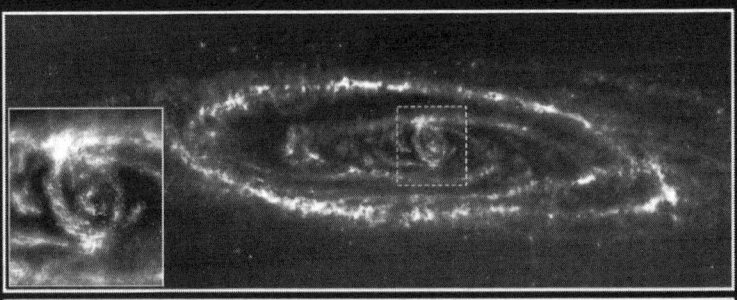

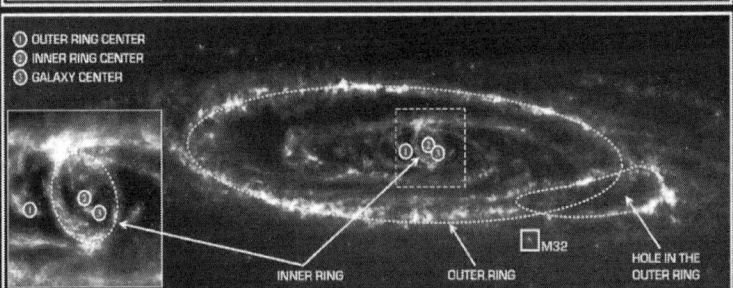

① OUTER RING CENTER
② INNER RING CENTER
③ GALAXY CENTER

INNER RING

OUTER RING

☐ M32

HOLE IN THE
OUTER RING

Dust in the Andromeda Galaxy   **Spitzer Space Telescope • IRAC**

NASA / JPL-Caltech / D. Block (Anglo American Cosmic Dust Lab, SA)   sig06-025

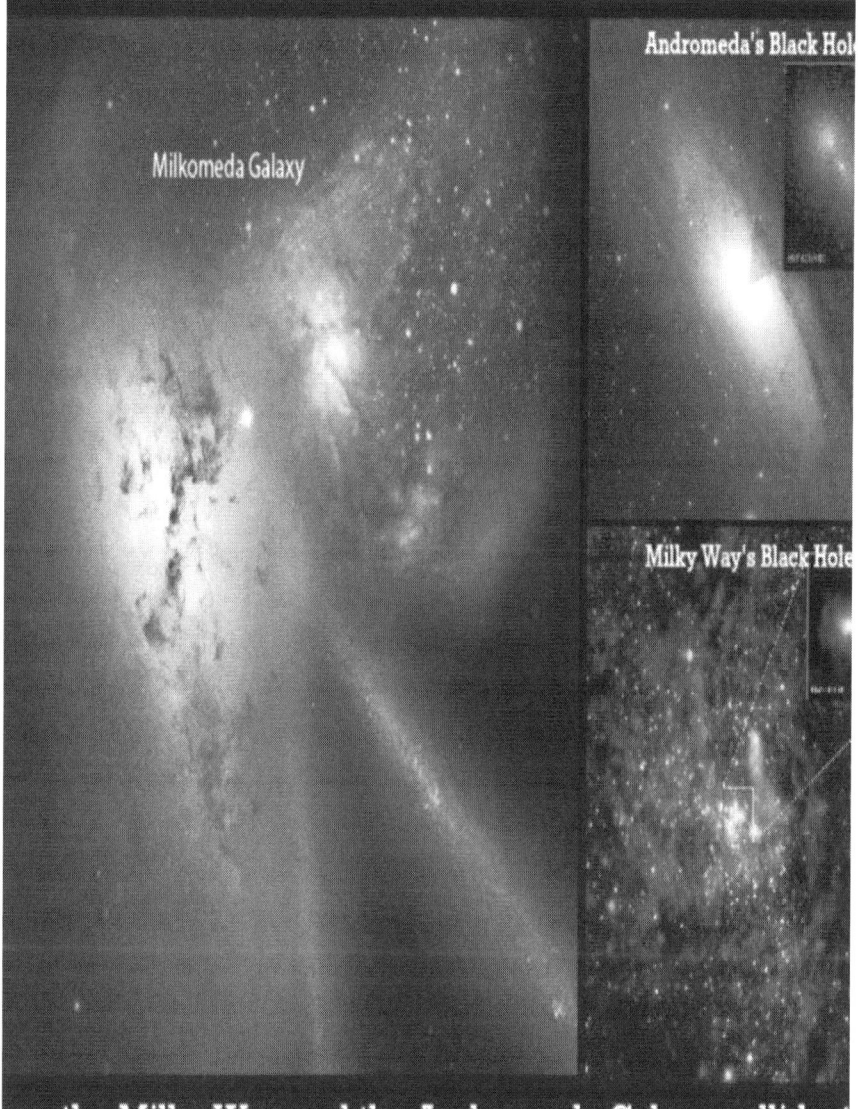

Milkomeda Galaxy

Andromeda's Black Hole

Milky Way's Black Hole

...hen the Milky Way and the Andromeda Galaxy collide, t... central black holes could merge to form a quasar.

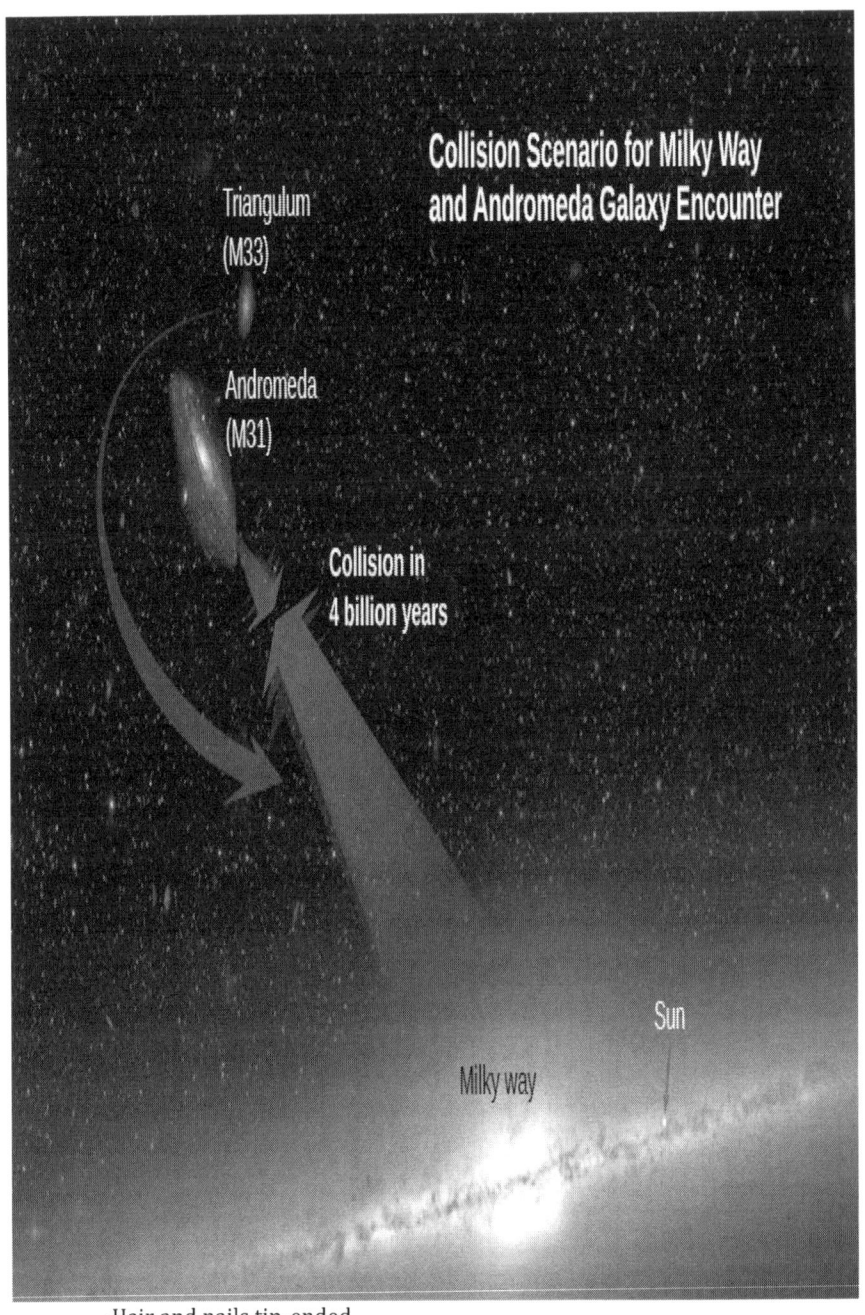

-Hair and nails tip-ended...

-*Arachnid* shell-encrusted finger nails knuckles...

Each of Us: *receding* remotely controlled motile-controlling motes

Autonomous spun-suction suppurating dis-charging *touching:*

      -Absolute-Zero…

      -The-Void.

      -Toward as away-from The Beginning…

      -The End!

      -EarthCentre!

      -Not-Yet!

Within and without drawn-into as out-of re-centring

Each and Every Other *whiff* and *whimsical* bloated-boated boasted suffrage.

Rotating roasting by role-rights and privileged-responses'

Squared triangulate Hexing Octagonal to The-Nines afloat anew:

      -The End of The Universe?

      -Not Yet.

      -Then. How? Known?

Each to Each-Other synced:

      -Gifted as Geneviève or Galahad! Aged-Giantine Galactic-Gallant…

      - Vortextual-Galactic guided…*floated Now*-Ourselves

As through and *over and under as dragged-into:*
      -Quasar-Ring Quintessence!

      -Celestial-Spheres!

      -Strange-Attractor…

Flattened-flat:

      -Great-Galactic…

      -Gravitational-Field…

      -The Great-Galactic-Ledge…

      -Edged! The Vertigo-Void! The End of Greatness!

      -Great Galactic-Wall Cosmic Microwave

Background:

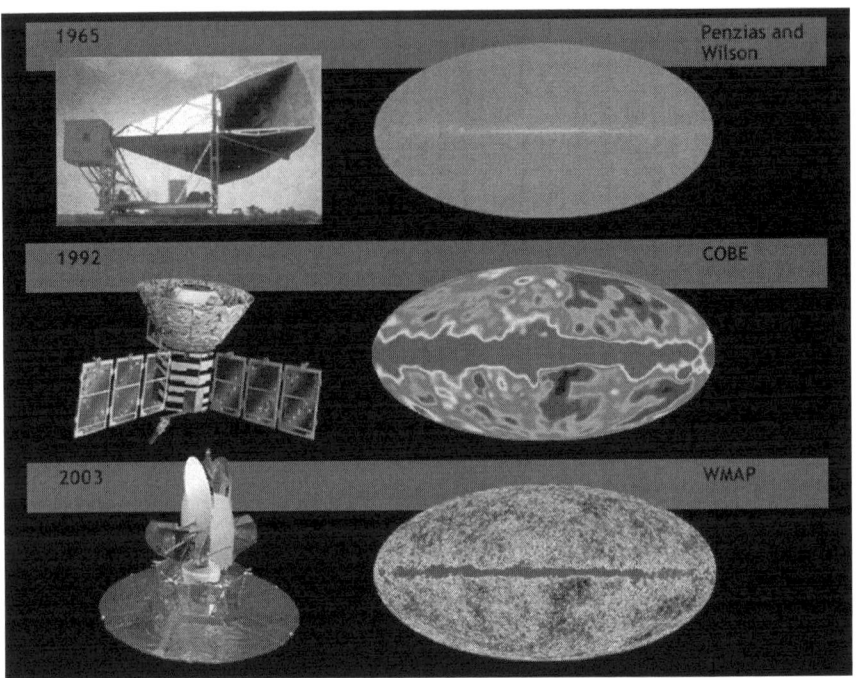

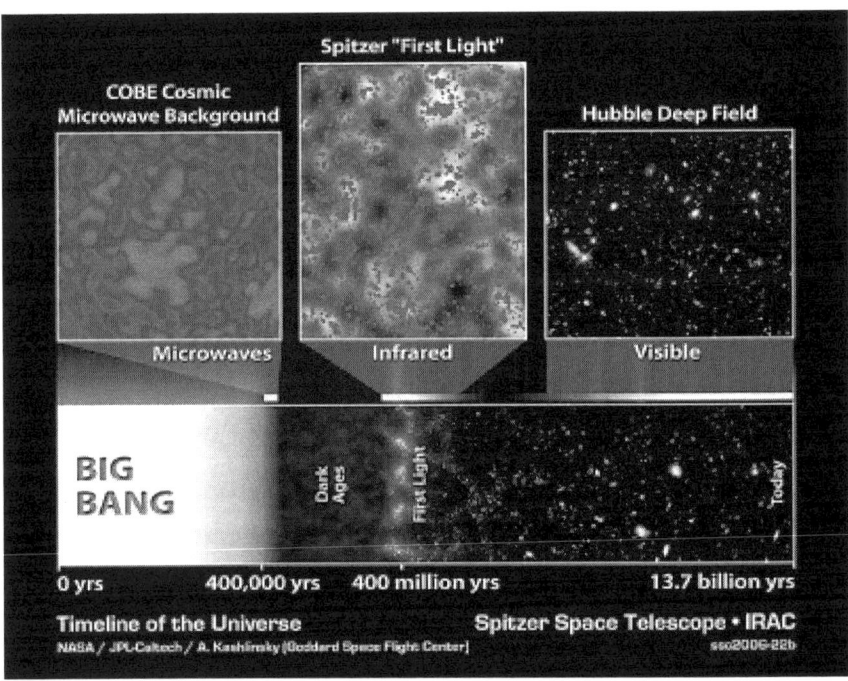

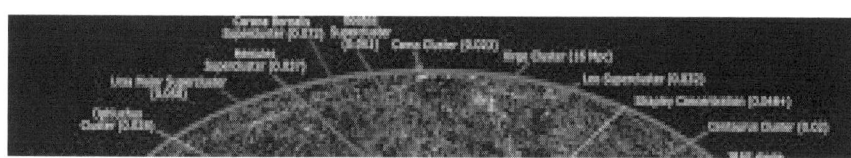

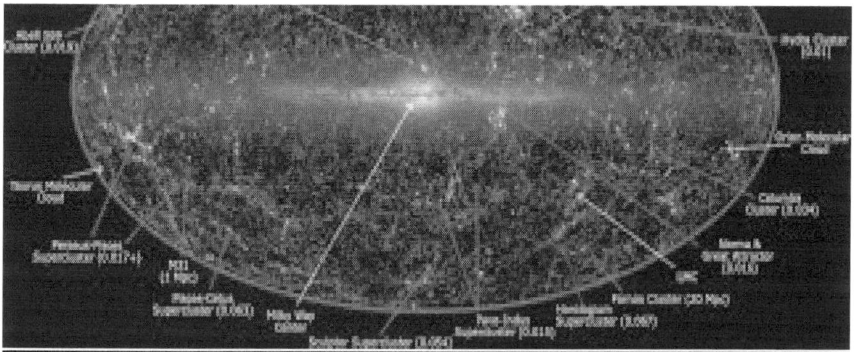

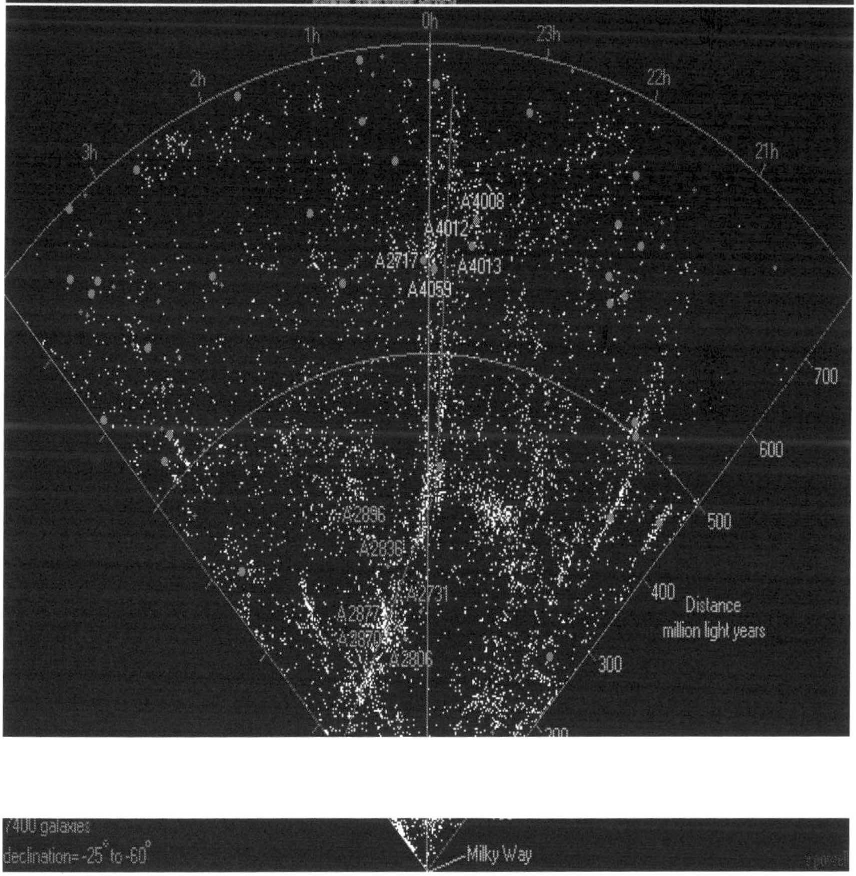
0h
1h
23h
2h
22h
3h
21h
A4008
A4012
A2717
A4013
A4059
700
600
500
A2896
A2836
A2731
400
Distance
million light years
A2877
A2870
A2806
300
200
7400 galaxies
declination=-25° to -60°
Milky Way

-White-Light?

-Dark-Light?

-Energy...*heat*...

Massively waning...

-Final-bounce...

-Last-*burn*...

As Each of Us:

-Atomic-molecular pullulating palpitating-clocks...

Docking:

-Wound-down de-regulating-axial abstemious...

-Cellular-operators...

-Mass as Energy-Producers...

-Digital-Constructors*...

-Di-polar dia-magnetic hadron-bosonic collided...no-more.

Seemingly fraudulent-forced fed forged germ-line:

-The un-familial as now familial...

-Pro-tonic electrical singular-points...

-Self-powering and flesh-protective colouring...

-Other-Islanded...

-Same Island now...

-Black-Hole!

-Non-Luminous! The-Universe itself!!

-Your-self!

-Ourselves!

Coiled-sprung barred bulging spiraling ponded and pondered:

-Life needs pain and *hunger*...

Producing headwaters contracting and extracted.

Spurted: Each of Us: starlight-innovator motivating-radiant.

Oceanic Galactic seas swam for our lives! Fearsome fleshed-out:

-EarthCentres...

Each relative-comparator to Each-Other hatched-twitching *twinkling*...

Allied Orbital imploded expanding-again with All-Else Zero'd:

-Out there!

-Here! Hyper-Noval Heroic! Super-Powers!!

Enclosing stringing-along yet separate-seeming whole-some...

Self-absorbing consuming flushed-out:

    -Mainframe Super-Processing...

    -Cyber-verse!

    -Tilting at Windmills...

    -Flooded drowned...

    -The Galaxies...

        -Stars'...

dying...

As sunken Treasure-Islanded.*

As consumed by light flushed-away in air...

As in water-refracting re-fracted:

    -As through this Universal-Space...

    -Life!

As glittering dust and gas cloned-crowing clowning perhaps yet still almost-spent.

Roughly-hewn principal-pieces coined closed-in

Each of Us freely roller-coastering riverboat showboat journeying

As through a now negatively-neutralizing neural-*nothingness*

1.8. Universal Galactic-Gallant.

Having decided.

This having been decided

At some point in the instantaneous and present-past willingly...

At some personal-point in the then future

Visiting EarthCentre and having taken all-necessary steps

In-principle cautionary against inevitable eventual in-iquitous failure.

Sooner than later than sooner

Dare-*devilling* work-force of brain and blood hearted and limbs agape

And by some seemingly sheer-chance combination of skill and luck, arrived.

Lately be-holden held-token holding-onto now

Steady-paced tensed and tension-*releasing...*

Toward and then beyond:

> -*This* Great-Galactic!

pausing...

> -Super-*stellar platform...*

> -*Hyper-Noval Ultra-Universe!*

> -As of Our-Selves!

> -Hyper-Massive planar-*scalar...*

> -Now! Greater than ever...

> -Special! Combined ever-expansive in all-directions...

> -This Universal Planar of travelling-direction forming out of *Nothingness...*

Auto-selected now within

The Full-Force Of linear-quadratic polar-equatorial.

Equational *moving*-functional atomic-circuitry...

Brightly and darkly-*surrounding* energetic-heaving:

> -The Centre of the Galaxy!

> -Galaxies. The-Universe...Hour-Glass:

> -Ourselves!

> -Other!

> -As Love and Hatred. Not. One without The-Other.

> - The Good and Bad...

Continuous sinuous-copious as:

> -*Hope and Faith...*

> -In Some Thing!

> -The Graces and Fates...

> -As Other the absence of The-One...

> -All!

As light and dark and everything between...

As at the very edge lit:

> -Black-Body *radiation...*

Darkly-immaterial and material *energetic* felt.

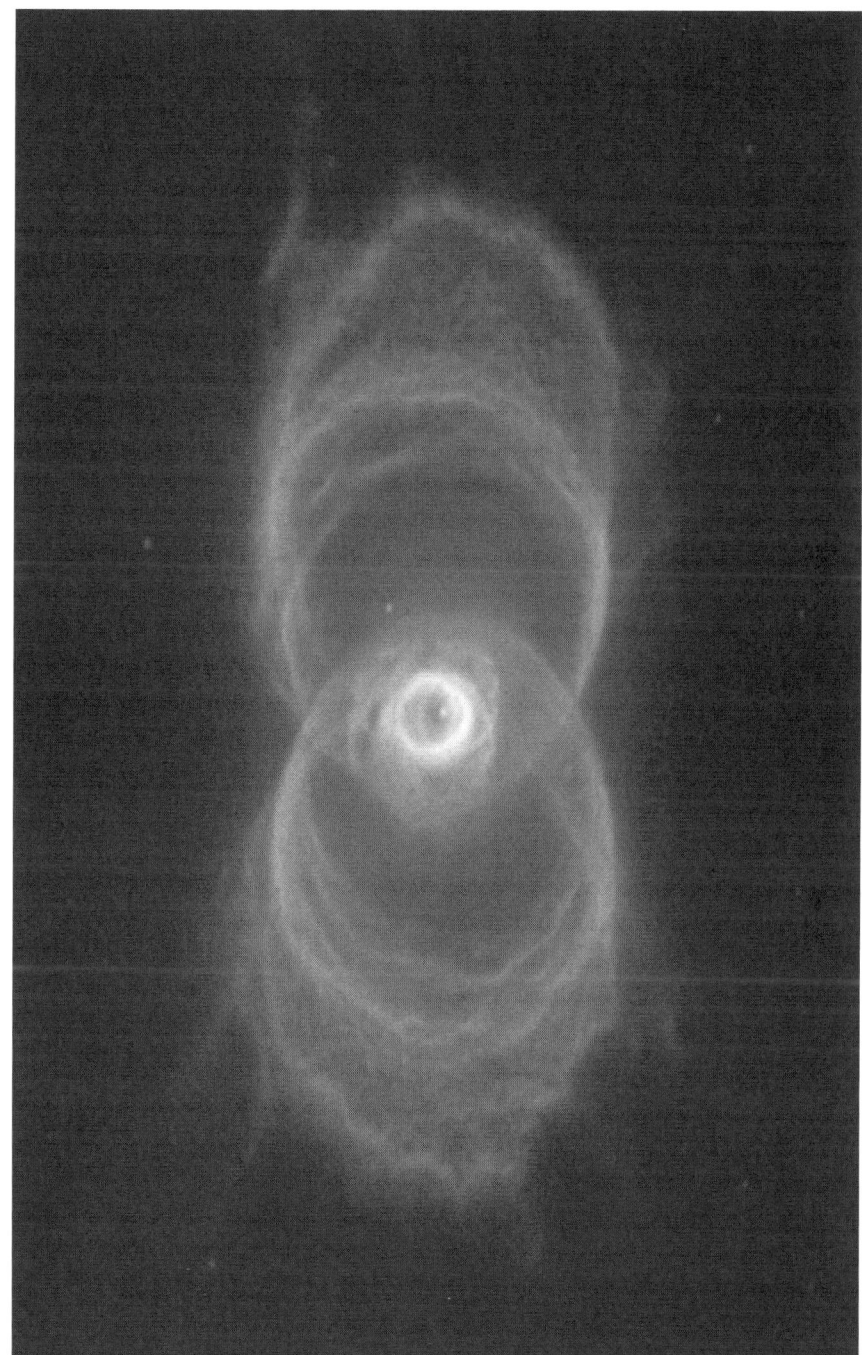

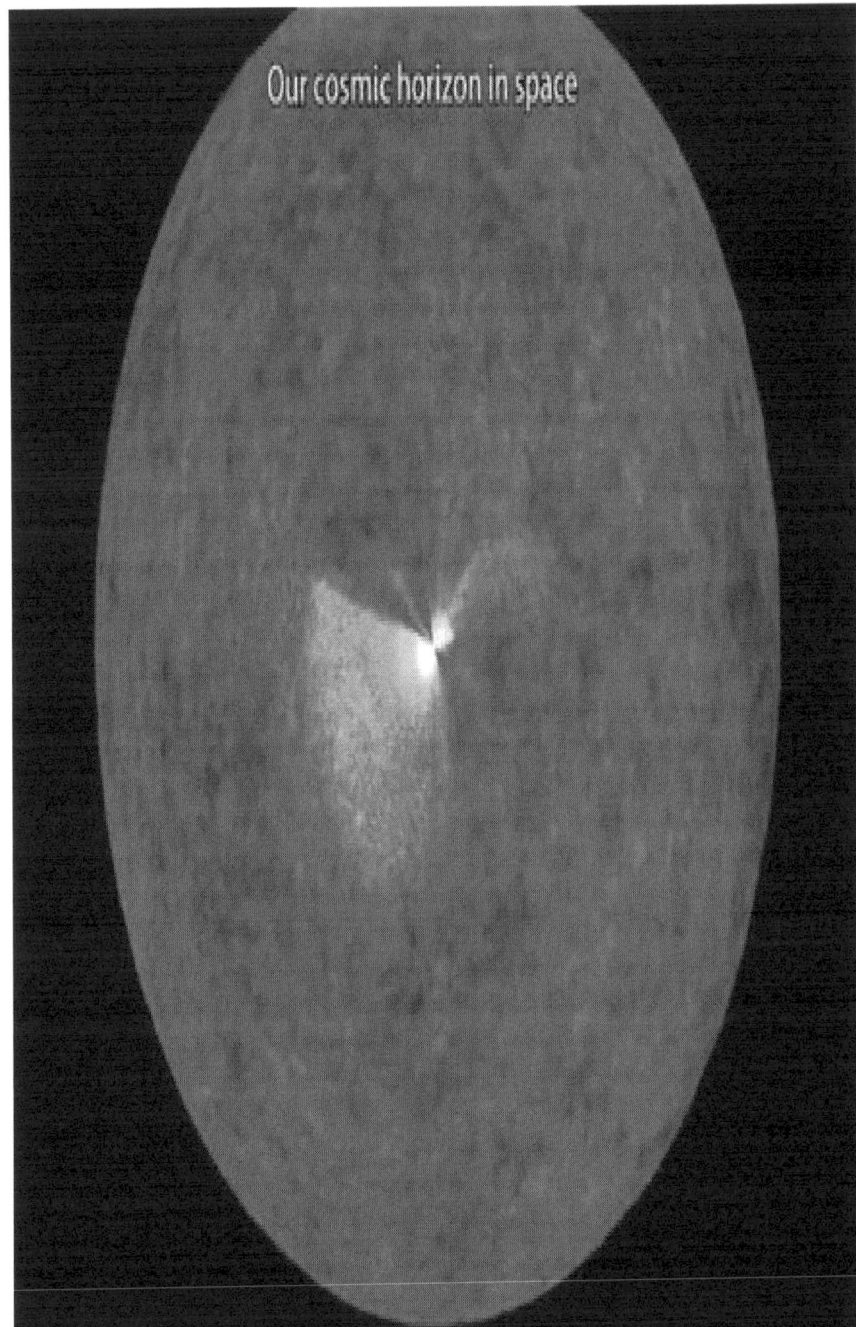

Seen and heard inseminate burned fused Gamite

Hapless-haploid diploid-zygotic

Gravity electronic-magnetic evolutionary bio-nucleic cells...

Amongst all-Other Outer to inner falling *ageing* cellular Star-mass.

As with Ourselves now:

> -Each of Each-Our-Selves...

> -Nucleating sprung from The Centre of The Galaxy!

> -Atomic-electronic computorial-*fundament...*

> *-Of The Universe... Ancient-Memories...*

Set-out in-motion fractionally fractally de-limiting

Curving-complex strapped-in.

As over another precipitous-edge landed-*amazed!:*

> -Ariadne-threaded labyrinthine...

> - The Sun-Queen*! mischievous King!

> -Strident Poseidon's Sea monstrous-raged...

Seemingly-*forever*:

> -Hydro-genous...

> -Andro-genius light –*flooded...*

> -Andromeda...

Saved!

> -As of Promethean-Perseus!

> -*Fire* stolen!

> -Pandorian-Hope!

> -No Hope of Hopeful-Heaven!

> -Or EarthCentre again!

> -Help! Hades! Galactic! Universal!

> *-Judgement-Day*:

Ledger-etched edged centring-edges lodged as equatorial-exacting.

Selected all-around:

> -Quadri-polar Quasar-Star!

> -Black-Hole

*meeting...*three-dimensional

steering

Moving four and more re-
moved:

-The Galactic-Centring...

      -Whole Brain! Faith! Hope! Whole! *Seemingly*...

      -All! Supernal-Circadian...

Hyper-massive gaping-privileged:

      -OurSelves!!

      -

As to the next and nearest and the largest

Mutant-melded re-molded *smoldering moldering*...

As at a raging Stygian Oceania-sired stirred

Acheronian petrified forest stumbled-into.

Crashed-into *landed* as a tsunami washed-inland.

As far as castellated *darkly* Universal-lit

As Over-Worlds and Under-Worlds of will and idea t*ilted-at:*

      -The Here and Now!

As held posed pared four-ways dimensional *moving*

Together:

      -Fatherless-Sons *returning*...

      -*Motherless-M*aidens...

      -Killing killed no more...

      -All-Other!

      -Mustard-seeded cabbage-brained!

De-fleshed leaved shredded and stalked:[*]

      -Seed to Seed! Brain being raining...

      -Alive! Sons and Daughters alike...

      -In-imical amicable loving faith...

      -Returning Super-Heroic!

      -Proteus!

      -Pan-Dora Hope!

Depleting...

      -Hope! Faith!

      -Infinitely! Lost...

      -Ex-Machina[*] Ended...

Awakened to dream-rescuing OurSelves and Each-Other:

    -Stellar Super-Massive...

    -Hyper-Galactic! Megalopolis!

    -Inter-stellar *re-forming* icy flaming-cometary:

    -Ovoid cepheid-centring *spiral*-unbarring *nucleic*-nest...

    -Stars and *then....*

    - The Galaxies mergent-*meet...*

Bi-optic skull-lensed *convergent as* spread-wings *gripped-on*

Each courted disaster-beyond snaked warping-bound:

    -Cosmic Super-Strings...

    -Ourselves!

    -Knotted.

    -Oscillate...

    -Good-*Vibrations!*

    -Far from War...

    -And everyday battles rock-islanded isolate.

    -Sunset horse-shoe Centaurean-hooves *headed...*

Riding-out strung-out bending bridging-saddled-with.

Tied-twisted curved and tightened-throughout

Heeled and toed tailing extruded:

    -Hyper-Spherical *prismatic...*

    -Squared-Spherinder...

    -Hyper-Cuboid 8-cell binary stellar-cellular fertile *fecund...*

    -De-centring emptying tri-point galactic nebulae...

Galactic-satellite sighting-sited and regressively-proportionate:

    -Universal Stellar-Planetary *ancient-starmass...*

    -Iron-nickel sulphurous-silicate core...

    -H*elium and hydrogen-linking* trailing dust and gas...

Universal Mega-Maser eyes paired energy-mass continuum *grinning...*

Outward inward-bound without Fates or *furious*-Graces.

Infernal-internal external-vengeance with-drawing

Blood and thought through-out:

    -The Kindly-Ones...Fury Fae...

Sandman: Neil Gaiman 1996 graphic novel. The Revenge of Gaia: James Lovelock 2000.

There and then:

       -The Universal-Skull!

Mouthing: in-vengeance punishing false-oath *loathing*-of:

Assuming of:

       -The Truth! Mother...

       -Pan-Demos!

       - Heavenly? -Father?

Wandering-Suns and Moons colliding breaking-off...

       -Paying-Foe! Almighty! Single-handed with Life-bribed in-debted debated

and unveiled-*threat*...

       -Abundance to and from The Grave *exchanged*...

       -*Lies, falsehoods and* - - Known

       u*ntruths...entanglement...chaos ensuing*

Realit(y)ies: forces between objects made of

smaller/larger combination inevitable

uniqueness amongst so-much variability ability

and false-reality past each momentary moment.

Reality-past alleged with blood sweat and tears

Dropped into an *endless* well of amative-sorority

Fraternal-sorrow and filial Loving-Life.

Tree-fallen monkey avatar-atman *scattered*

Killed for killing

Feuding endless-revenge ended.*

Forever now only family-feeding invisible fingers and hands and legs

Wrought distraught limbic-*wringing*...

Attempting-arachnoid anechoic-fell ever *attempted* re-climbing too-late.

Cumbrous-*lustrous* grabbing greedy yet *icy*-watery iconic-ion contrail-wheeling.

Carbon-steeling:

       -Mono-chromatic electro-magnetic...

-Specto-scopic frequency as wavelength gravitational-saved!

-Sceptred-Keyed…

-Games of Thrones! Persephone! Termagant

-(R)E-galitarianism transcendent and immanent *ultimate*-Reality…

-Supreme Cosmic Spirited remote *Starlight*-Common's-*Wealth:*[*]

-Super Universal HyperNoval…

-Galactic Green Dragon-Fly…

tiny gravity string loops smooth and

continuous gravity quantum-lumps

holographic imprint onto a two

dimensional surface

(there is no such thing).

Emergent time-space-temperature

Boost hotter and hotter through

Absolute-Zero Space. Pre-dicting

Place position-Planet

Probabilities to future expected

outcomes bias-based always

Constructors, is what we are…

Possible.

Behaviours in Quantum-fields

determined-by: fishes in a pond, many

fishes in many ponds…

inferring-realities'

from realities

from realities

 from realities…

-Vicious-Vixen Wolverine!

Dolphin and The Rats Brigades as Centaurean-*pulling:*

-The Galaxies!

-By Sacrificial-*Savagery!*

Put-out. Super-massive ever more ancient rock-cloud from *emptiness...*

-*Super-ficial...*

-*Nothingness...*

Radio-emission switched-on then off.

Spiralling-inward Out-of-Control *whited* flashed!

And now All as Solar-setting centring-*eclipsing:*

-Disruptive*

-Purposeful...

-Hopeless...

-Universal-Life Force...

-The Centre of The Galaxies...

Finally as taken as denied:

-Our-Selves!

Amplified -gravity re-duced micro-wave molecular macro-
radiant. Pin-wheeling drawn-in sumped-inward as pumped-up.

Blown-inward planetary-lunar colliding-collapsing

Universal population propulsion *inversion*-convergent

Stinging then as once-sung singed as before:

-Optimally-heated de-optionally re-absolute *frozen*:

-To: The End of The Universe!

As seen through:

-The Reflection:

-Of All-Galaxies into One.

Scraping-sided scoping barely coping now

Darkly and *lightly* cellular-capped plodded-podded.

De-Linking chained parallel-caged and in final-collision razoring-laser lettered
Pen-ultimate Universal-thresholds met.

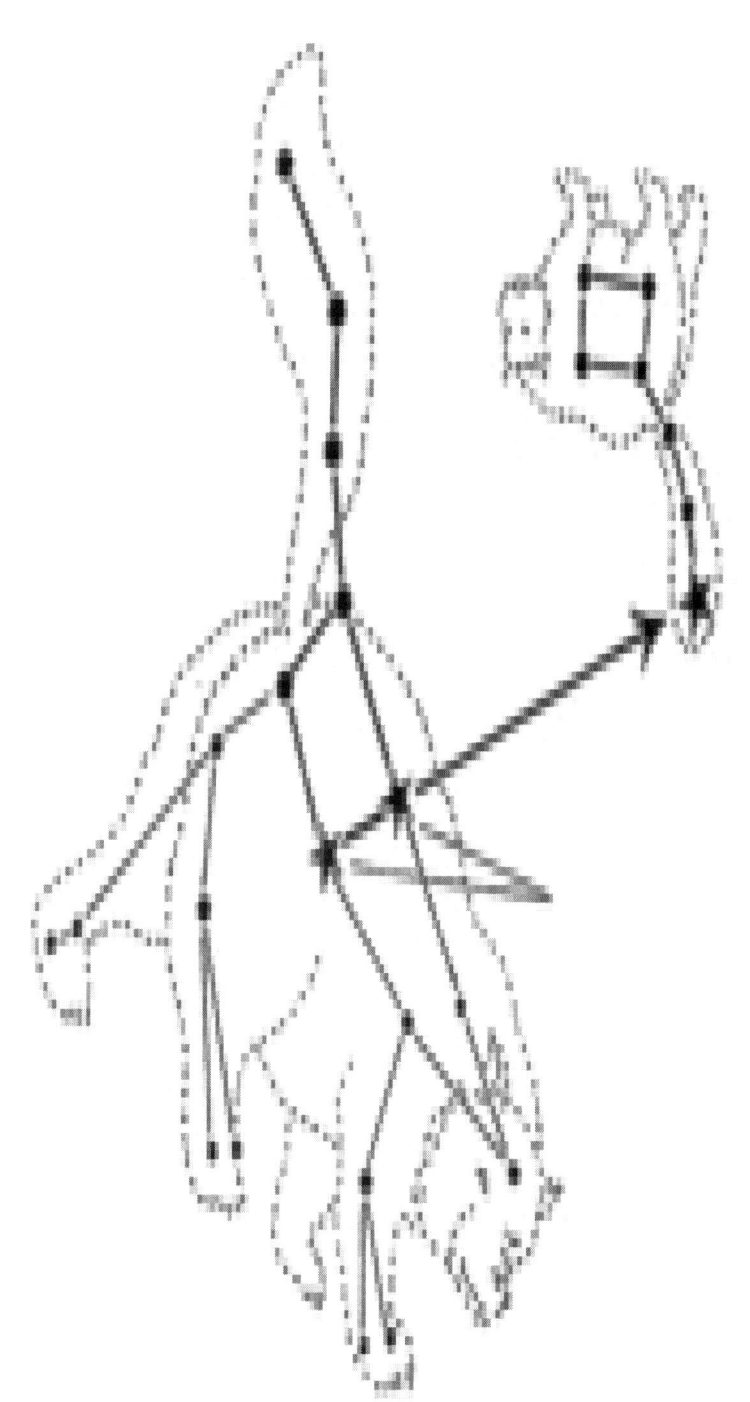

Great and not so great Ursa-Bears* berserkers sewn-up hounded and devoured-devout

Minotaur-mazed meeting vacuum-vortex mutinous-murderous

Devious gravity nucleate-wave accumulate string-strung strongly-*weakly*

Electro-magnetic: thrashed-out returning finally conclusively-*sunken* downed drowned

Suffocating:

      -All-Other Galactic drawn-in...

      -Re-combing combining re-pairing conal-centering *vortextual...*

      -We!

      -The third-greatest of: The-Local Galaxies...

      -Quadri-Polar!

      -Hyper-spherical...

      -Quantum-Quasar...

      -Quark! Universal-Galaxy! Home!

      -EarthCentre?

      -Protean!

      -Neutron!

      -*Neutronium...*

Spiraling Cosmic-curling

De-furling...

      -Prometheus!

      -Andromeda!

      -Triangulum*!

Continued...

EndNotes/ summary:

[*] Terrible Tree. Norse/German mythology as Yggdrasil. The World or Life Tree as linking to the sky and at the Earth and rooted in water wells of Wisdom (Graces) and Fates (Destiny) boiling raging roaring *furious* rivers (The Furies of judgement and justice, self-conscience and social retribution) to The End of Days (the ultimate battle of The Gods and mortal beings at Ragnorak, the End War) when in flames of the dead as leaves from The Tree in autumn and winter frozen over are as the bodies of the dead washed up from the seas, and The Gods (including Odin and Freya, and the trickster Loki) exiled forever to the skies and humanity left alone, to our own devices. The Tree of Life also appears in ancient Chinese and Mayan/Aztec/Inca mythology, inhabited by feeding fish and fowl, serpent, dragons and phoenix bird stood in an endless river well (The UnderWorld) cyclically in the Sanskrit/Hindu scripture to the fourth final Kali Yuga, or End of Strife and Abrahamic Bible as World Axis. Mythical ending all war between Gods and Man. As Ragnorak (Norse Twilight of The Gods). The Sanskrit Mahabharata account of the devastating Krishna/Kurukshetra war's ending, by Krishna breathing winds of life. Modern religious and political warfare including wars of conquest and Empire from, and across all continents, since ancient times, for land, and wealth.

[*] All exclamations! and use of personal pro-nouns and capital initials here purposefully used for emphasis, personal effect, and connection e.g. One/I; as generally sparingly used by Walt Whitman (Leaves of Grass/Song of Myself (1855)): 'I believe a leaf of grass is no less than the journeywork of the stars...I am as one disembodied, triumphant, dead.' Also anthropocenic and science convention, as literarily named: Our: The Earth, The Sun, The Galaxy, The Universe.

[*] Darwin (George) The (lunar) Tides and Kindred Phenomena of The Solar System (1899).

[*] As Alice in Wonderland: Lewis Carol: 1865; The Universe as The Pool of Tears; or The Caucus Race going around in circles, with no end. So, all are declared winners simply for being there and then. Also: Chinese myth of Chang'e The Rabbit Moon Goddess banished to the sky forever with Yi the Sunbird.

[*] Universal Abyss. Olaf Stapledon: Starmaker (1937): 'Sitting there on the heather, on our planetary grain, I shrank from the abysses that opened up on every side and into the future'. Fast radio burst neutron star quantum gravity effects are known as 'burping' black-holes.

[*] The Universe: as an inflating filled vacuum negatively neutrally false-positively occupied from the Big -Bang and continuous steady-state emergence of membrane strings in space and time, as variant oblate bubble and increasingly vast widening inflationary gravitational gaps (vacua) between nucleating electro-magnetic energy-mass and centring object black-holes (non-luminous stars: neutron-electron/proton) all cosmological objects (luminous energy-mass stars) moving away from, as towards each other due to the originating curvature of space and time (Newton-Einstein-Hubble) cosmic gravitational energetic forces forming mass and eventually self/other evolutionary-being through adaptive switching automotive selective will and power relationship.

*Coleridge-Taylor: Rime of the Ancient Mariner (1798). Moral aloneness in nature. Morality in retrospect of the done and irreversibility of action (such as marriage/childbirth) of maturity, and learned wisdom in advance of such action.

* As T.S. Eliot: The Wasteland (1922) ritual romantic life and Earthly/Godly betrayal as the biblical Apocalypse, pointlessness, impotence, and loss of faith in family and a necessarily goodly (human) nature (e.g. through unrequited love, war). Four Quartets (1943): 'Other *echoes* inhabit the garden.' (thought/mind/personal-moment/memory/tradition/culture).

* Laozi: Tao: Dao Te Ching. 5-6th Century Before the Modern Era. The Way: of personal virtue/goodness inner strength of character and existential integrity, towards self and All Other(s). Aristotle's Ethics: naturally deliberate action aiming imaginatively at the good (outcome) explanation, including utilitarian happiness (of the individual/many/most).

* Rachel Carson marine-biologist: The Edge of The Sea (1955): 'The micro-droplet of water separating one grain of sand from another is like a vast dark sea'. The Silent Spring (1962); E.O Wilson: Consilience (1998) combining Earthscience: psychology, physics and chemistry, socio-biology.

* Ask(m) and Embla(f) are the (Norse) mythic first mortals on Earth, revealed/born from ash/elm trees/nature (Edda prose/poem: Snorri Sturlusson (Norse 13th century).

* Bladerunner film 1982 Ridley Scott. 'May computer robots assume human imagination emotion or selective generational evolutionary choice based on General Artificial Intelligence?' Do Androids Dream of Electric Sheep? (Science fiction novel: Phillip K. Dick. 1968.)

* This Sporting Life; novel by David Storey (1963; film Lindsay Anderson). Incompatible public sporting (successful celebrity) and private personal complex family and love lives.

* The Universal-Skull: the two larger and smaller Magellanic hydrogen cloud-galaxies (eyes) with The–Galaxy as a toothed-grin below, as seen only from the Southern hemisphere.; the centaurian and scorpion constellations at the centre of The Galaxy of aged dying stars circling a hyper-massive black-hole beyond which the zone of avoidance or indifference, or visible exclusion area, Great Galactic Wall.

Pan-Gou (China) and Ymir (Norse) are northern hemisphere mythological equivalents, embodying of The Earth hills and trees, and mindful skies, as if all seeing (as Greek Gods from Mount Olympus); The Universe as a stellar mind-map limbic optical neural-synaptic nervous-system, as through global animist anthropic mythology legend and religion/ Universal Life-Principle. The Existential-Anthropocentric.

* The Cosmological Principle as viewed on a sufficiently large scale, the properties of The Universe are the same for all observers. JAXA (Japanese) Suzaku satellite X-ray telescope / Stanford University (USA) Simionescu et al. 2015 indicates the average atomic content of Galaxies and stars, including The Sun, and OurSelves, are similar to less than a 10% variation across The Universe overall. The cosmic similarity of atomic nucleus and surrounding electron shell and solar-system is known as The Planetary Atomic Theory first proposed by Maria Meyer (1906-1972).

* Indication of how The Earth may be eventually be destroyed and/or self-destruct from within; be blown out of the Solar-System by the expanding Sun, or sucked outward with the expanding Universe, or inward to the centre of The Galaxy, with other ageing and dying stars. We anyway conjecturally to be returned to black-holes as at the centre of atoms (neutrons/quarks) them/Our Selves who may be uniquely situated as life forms in The Universe. To effect/affect slowly or more quickly differing degrees of evitability, through will-power and conscious manipulation of

mathematical geometric expectation or probability functions of space and time, with intended, and un-intended consequences.

*Confucius (551-479 Before ME) personal/societal secular existential humanism as exemplified in moral parable and expected duties of and towards Other. Especially, the duty of the ruler/family head, to feed and maintain social and family life as the ethically good within self and society. A relative perceptual moral dualistic Yin/Yang (shadow/light) in contrast to absolute non-complementary Oneness in/of The Universe. Eternal change and necessarily balanced judgement as the questioning Confucian/Socratic method, taking in differing relative or absolute assumed viewpoints, and authoritarian (by reasoned argument) and democratic social and political decision-making.

* Plato: Diogenes: Man(is) neither God, nor a featherless bipedal chicken, only ever able to seek ideal perfection (or philosophical understanding/definition of good love beauty truth etc.). Edgar Allan Poe: Eureka! (1848) detective-ratiocination; Raising the Wind: diddling considered as one of the exact sciences (1843). Man (as of or any God) as the hoaxer or author or interpreter self as other deluding in a game of life (in respect of unfair unethical immoral advantage, enrichment, usury, superiority).

OurSelves each as a centre of momentum/mass inertial frame in which we each are a relativistic quantum atomic unique originating physical point, unable to achieve or imagine ideal perfection, but possibly be close enough to the assumed ideal in a sufficiently if not necessary good life; choice and freedom of the existential-self in integral good faith in ourselves and others; gender/ post-colonial ethnicity/ myth and religiosity: Sartre/ Fanon/ Beauvoir (The Ambiguity of Ethics 1945)/Iris Murdoch).

* Boethius: The Consolation of Philosophy (6th C Modern Era): the nature of an amoral and immortal God with fore-knowledge (determinism) as compatible with mortal free-will and personal/social responsibility. God, as an immortal and amoral spectator to mortal actors observed in life; OurSelves then being existentially of, and for OurSelves, without foreknowledge, having relative free-will and ability to change, adapt and alter our ways through shared personal and social moral responsibilities.

* The (Heisenberg/ Schrodinger) uncertainty indeterminacy principle in quantum mechanics, as to the non-absolute therefore relative probability functions of complementary variables, such as position, distance, time, mass and space and perspective; 1-n-body problem in gravitational theory (Newton) and practice, related to cosmological objects and electrical-magnetic potential; nucleate/particulate atomic quantum and chaos theory (Poincare maps; Lorenz transformations (butterfly effect); Mandelbrot fractals).

* Natural Observable Universal Law/Golden Rule: A basic probative or directive always to be followed to ensure evolutionary success/continuation. Universal-Star/Global-Sun deity (Egyptian Ra) and New Testament imperative to : 'do as you would be done by'. Old Testament (Jeremiah): '...for I will forgive their iniquity, and I will remember their sin no more'. Mercy. Good/Evil as of both light and darkness (shadow). In social evolutionary terms that wrong (violence/ murder/rape/ extortion/lying/ stealing/ theft) is generally known and avoided, and through
free-will generally avoidable. in order to avoid suffering, or as such sin being done to one's own self in return; and not due necessarily to clerical or legal advice, but social deterrence (torture, death penalty, deliberate punishment) as a personal individual drive (religious worship/respect) and natural aversion linked to empathy and the notion of equal or reciprocal fair play, through balancing possible payback, or dis-regard (and not pure altruism) as in social-scientific game play.

* 'No man (or women) chooses evil because it is evil; s/he only mistakes it for happiness, the good s/he seeks.' Mary Woolstencraft; from A Vindication of the Rights of Woman: with Strictures on Political and Moral Subjects (1792).

* Plato: The Republic/Phaedo: cave-sun/shadow shadow-allusion. As Universal Space beyond while on Earth the whole of humanity are in less than perfect ideal circumstances, understanding or morality except possibly through anthropic evolutionary reason logic and existential good faith (Lao-zi/Aristotle/Kant/Sartre).

* Virginia Woolf: To The LightHouse (archetypal stream of consciousness novel:1927): The complexity of experience and (all) relationships, compassion and social conscience morality and amorality: 'For now she need not think of anybody. She could be herself, by herself. And that was what now she often felt the need of - to think; well not even to think. To be silent; to be alone. All the being and the doing, expansive, glittering, vocal, evaporated; and one shrunk, with a sense of solemnity, to being oneself, a wedge-shaped core of darkness, something invisible to others... and this self having shed its attachments, was free for the strangest adventures.'

* Minkowski-Feynmann diagrams (1908-1985) atomic-framed hyperbola-space with quantum-mechanics and electronics described as diagrammatic interstices, stick-like 4-limbed figures describing quasar-quark stars as cyber-physical representations. Penguin diagram (Mary K. Gaillard; Melissa Franklin; John Ellis; Dmitri Nanapoulos) of charge conjugation parity-variation.

* The waterfall illusion (Aristotle) of water falling and solid rock appearing as if rising, with the feeling of vertigo or dis-equilibrium, sea-sickness, or social Nausea(Sartre 1938). The un/real true-feeling indescribable ultimately, that all solid objects are moving relative to each and all other.

*Calculus: differential integral equations curving or sloping space/volume and change variation (time and space) in maths geometry and algebra. Method of limiting exhaustion or boundary conditions of infinitesimals/probability/heuristics (Archimedes;Liu Hui; Al-hazen; Leibniz; Newton; Lorenz; et al science/mythology)

* The Naturalistic Fallacy (G.E. Moore Principia Ethica 1903) proposes pragmatic practical social morality (goodness) against the tendency to attribute actions reductively to natural desires or emotions as naturally ethically knowable/unavoidable or neutral (such as killing for food or in self-defence, or a generalised personal wish for happiness. A Universe being neutral or non-moral being (Hume 1740) raising the 'is-ought' or 'could/should' problem of personal and social ethics. The naturalistic fallacy is a tendency of those who attribute empirical scientific or religious ethicism, or use evolutionary science as a reason for all and especially otherwise inexcusable actions, avoidability or avoidable selfish actions such as extreme violence, lust and greed.

* Free-radicals are unstable atoms with an unpaired outer-electron that must through magnetic attraction/distraction gain or lose an electron, through atomic-stabilising nuclear-gravitational reaction. Social political radicals are similarly on the outside of society (Camus: The Outsider 1958).

*Murray Gell-Mann and George Zweig (1960) and Geoffrey Chew (1966) quanta variation-response and bootstrap quantum-dynamics. Lev Landau (1951) Feynmann (1949) density-state particle-ontology with hierarchical mis-match and alter(able democratic non-autocratic critical mass inter/intra-dependency of all parts of any energy-mass equation (in motion thus perspective/probability).

* As Bottichelli's painting The Birth of Venus. The Platonic ideal or Divine Spirit and Earthly physical subjectivity (beauty outwardly and inwardly to the beholder and the beheld) combining perceived familiarity in Platonic beauty, love and The Good (in ethics/morality/social politics). Diego Rivera: Man at The Crossroads/Centre of The Universe: mural 1933-4 Mexico.

* An EarthCentre Light Year: is the speed and distance light can travel in one Solar orbit/year (approx. 9 trillion kilometres) with wavelength light sound and radio-extremes from Absolute-Zero to the current known mini/max speed of light/heat in hot-cold *oscillating* Space in all direction/dimensions the same.

* Darwin (Charles): The Descent of Man (1871) The phrase 'survival of the fittest' has been mis-used as an assumed 'Law of the Jungle' or survival of the strongest; whereas it is apparent that the strongest are more usually less likely to survive or reach old age, and more likely be short lived than the weaker who generally through democratic majority and reduced social risk-taking share avoidance of violence and greed, or all out individualistic hedonism (Nietzsche) for a shared and general satisfaction in social togetherness and more likely shared numerical survival e.g. both animal and genders generally engage in protective family/herd social behaviour (Beauvoir The Second Sex, 1949). *One is not born, but rather becomes, a woman.*
All oppression creates a state of war. One's life has value so long as one attributes value to the life of others, by means of love, friendship, indignation and compassion. Representation of the world, like the world itself, is the work of men; they describe it from their own point of view, which they confuse with the absolute truth. Fe-males more by perceived threat (fright) and gifting (favour) freeze or fainting, or feigning; rather than sado-masochistic actual combat (fight) or abandonment (flight). Neuro-science stresses acute response in gender studies, with variant degrees of nature/nurture through cultural generational as well as individual desires, emotions, and designs.

* Absolute-Zero -375 degrees Celsius: the established. Initial temperature of the early Universe. The Cosmic Background Radiation is currently -270 degrees Celsius averaged out and cooling rapidly following the standard Big Bang model. Cosmic Inflation (Hubble) is estimated to have shown approx. 1000 trillion Celsius-degrees in the hottest earliest most-aged stars (at the centre of The Galaxy). The discovery of measurable stellar atomic radiation is attributed to Marie Curie (1867-1934) and Chien Shiung Wu (1912-1974) for parity variation, violation, decay, entropy.

* Loop-quantum super-string gravity composite molecular compounds, with proportionate plurality (and dis-proportionate conflict and self-destruction resolutions) at the molecular cellular generational levels, resembling iconoclastic political autocracies that may lead to massive democratic deficit or deviation. Day to day experience suggests relatively harmless cautious daily battles of life require social harmony not perpetual conflict to succeed/survive indefinitely: Confucius' balanced bureaucratic state; Henry Thoreau: Walden; or A Life in The Woods (1854). Humanity as needing to respect and learn through nature, mindfulness as spirit or soul sharing nature and not apart; as spontaneous transformations and oneness within nature (as weather/meteorology). United Nations 1942: Roosevelt/Churchill/Litvinov/ Soong and the recognition and overview of Universal Human Rights.

* The Anthropic Life-Principle: *conditions that are observed in the universe must allow the observer to exist (Merriam-Webster dictionary).* Humanity occupies a privileged position in the Universe due to existing co-incidental selection of numerical relations between altering cosmological constants, especially the epochal evolution of main-sequence stars (Penrose: The Emperors New Mind, 1989)

and the mere fact of our existence as necessitating Self as Other preservation through conscious actions as well as unconscious and at times unconscionable murderous instinct; countered through a deliberate practical morality, and eventual inevitable suicide, as Our cells systematically destroy each other as OurSelves *themselves*; excepting only, perhaps, in the immediate and lasting immediate memory.

* Pan (oply): vessel; move across look, gaze, array, film; criticise/judge all; also as Pan-chronican (time travel); Panoplaic (as at play; suit of armour/splendid display); Pan God (Greek) of wild nature and fertility and originating of humanity (Chinese: Pan Gou). Female as TanGou or Tannit (Phoenician: Carthage North African Berber Mother Goddess of Skies and as Minerva/Saturn and completing the Greek/Roman triumvirate of Zeus/Jupiter and Hera. In Punic culture TanGou/Tannit is represented as a trapezium (Triangulum).

* Love's Labours Lost: Shakespeare (1564-1614 plays): unrequited love/life as comedy and tragedy.

* As Homer (850 BME: The Odyssey/Iliad: mythical Odysseus: sailing into the sunset, to war; home to Penelope and their unknown son, Telemachus (far from war); as Tennyson (Roman: Ulysses (Oddyseus)1842): 'To follow knowledge like a sinking star, beyond the utmost bound of human thought.'

* Earth and Venus (Indo-European mythology mother/daughter) quartery of inner-rocky planets with Mars (father/son) and Mercury (Underworld/retrograde warning messenger). The four outer-Giant gas and then ice-rock planets have also (likely) iron-rich heaviest first-stage atomic stellar nucleation originating asteroidal cores, axially accreting gases minerals and heavy metals and are cosmological objects named and linked with ancient and modern world myth and legend as this text and e.g. Japanese Manga: Naoko Takeuchi: Sailor Moon 1991 and modern geologic-archaeological, anthropological, astro-physical and quantum-atomic and cosmological observation.

* Wiccan Rede (European early and later pagan: road/path/advice): 'Do what you will that none are harmed.' as Buddhist teaching and The Hippocratic Oath in medicine; also: The Golden Bough: 1890 James Frazer: to 'Do no harm'. Conversely: To do to others as you would have done to yourself: as The Ethic of Reciprocity or The Golden Rule (almost) ubiquitous as a personal and social functionality across all religions and secular global ethics, and implicates the biblical eye for an eye, tooth for a tooth (rendering all blind, toothless (voiceless) and unfeeling of the truth; fighting fire with fire, flood with water. To do to Others as They would do to you, implies that if you believe your enemy will harm you then you may harm them (even pre-emptively, firstly, and through possibly endless escalation); whereas to avoid all harm, implies being kind even to your enemies, but risks their potential harm to yourself, and which therefore seems irrational, and instinctively unnatural. However, these examples of game-play essentially require judgement, and justification, with diplomatic and democratic min/max . alternatives to fighting, flight, or fright. Special pleading perhaps, mercy, forgiveness and other self and shared –interpretation.

* Jupiter and Saturn are modernly thought to be failed Suns, forming Giant dust and gas cloud planets. The difference of which to the Solar System, Earth, and OurSelves questions how or if we would have existed in a triple or binary Sun system?; if we/life had existed on Earth then at all? Would the circum-solar habitable zone have been habitable (Goldilocks hypotheses) with neither too hot nor too cold parameters? Do other such Earthlike habitable planets exist, or life exist within different parameters of life as we know it on Earth, elsewhere on Earth, or The Universe?

* Hero(Greek Priestess original hero/ine) and Leander(Man/Lion) at Hellespont: Hero's lighthouse beacon beckons Leander in a storm swimming to her to procreate, yet to his death by drowning. Hero in despair then threw herself from the tower into the sea, also to drown; as Shakespeare's Romeo and Juliet, and countless other World myth and legends, of forewarned disallowed love and death/loss.

* Genetic sibling children have been known to find each other and consort readily in adulthood; only if un-known to each other growing-up. Siblings or cousins growing-up together, have a known aversion to such sibling incest throughout the animal world (The Westermark Effect: or reverse psycho-sexual imprinting/pheromonal attraction, learned revulsion).

* In global myth and psycho-analysis, a warning against incest and immortality through death and death-denial/immortality (Freud/ Jung/Becker/Campbell) . Universal social token and taboo across all cultures. Inner/outer crime of passion and detection in literature (Maureen Murdock: The Herione's Journey (1990)). Infelicitous infidelity leading to error and treachery.

* Vayu-Mudra are elegant and beatific hand-gestures used in Yoga and a slow Indo-European dance (Pavane) as purifying spiritual-channelling and healing-balance complementing dark and light; good/evil truth/falsity as Yin and Yang: dialectic thesis/anti-thesis synthesis (Hegal/Marx), non-absolute duality, or continuum dividing and multiplying continuously throughout the cosmos. Chinese Hun (Yin/mind/cloud or shadow spirit) and Po (Yang/body/corpse) sharing elements in life, separated in death not necessarily in an afterlife, but for ancestral remembrance/worship. Many cultures have many more distinctions than the simple dualistic, and varied spirit souls (for example, Innuit have separate spirit souls for respiration and digestion, and other bodily and worldly natural functions and experiencing senses as now brain/neuron like structures attached to other bodily organs, including sensory organs, digestive and sexual. (Heribert Watzke TED talks 2010).

* Atman/Avatar/Monkey-God (ancient China/India) Mytheme (Levi-Strauss; Propp; Dennett; Manovich) shared source/narrative: Society as Super-Organism and Global/Universal brain (skull)/hive mind (Aristotle; Hobbes; Emerson; E.O. Wilson; Lynne Margulis (MicroCosmos; with Dorion Sagan 1986); Vladimir Vernadsky (1863-45) Institute of Geo-Chemistry. The human brain has 100 billion neurons each neuron connected to 10 thousand other neurons: 'Sitting on your shoulders is the most complicated object in the known Universe' Michio Kaku. The Future of The Mind 2014. HyperSpace: A Scientific Odyssey 1994.

* Orion's Belt and Taurus constellations. Babylonian Heavenly Shepherd. Egyptian King/God Osiris. Arabic:al-Jabbar: The Giant. Hungarian Nimrod magic archer or reaper. Norse Freya weaving distaff. Sanskrit sacred Deer Mriga. Native American Bison. Australia Cooking Pot. Meso-American pigs. hearth-home Blood Women or ball Game-Players. Inca Three Worlds or family. Aztec Fire-Drill Trapezium. Greek myth placed by Zeus (Roman: Jupiter) amongst the stars with Taurus Bull (Celtic divine Bull with Three Cranes) ruled by Venus/Aphrodite/Hera (Roman Juno wife and sister of Zeus), the Egyptian goddess Isis and god Pan. Orion and Taurus are the most easily recognized constellations of both hemispheres, and represent generally animist religious familial love food and war (the hunt). African Chinese and many others: Heavenly House with siblings/family.

* Gryphon: with the head and wings of an eagle and the body and tail of a lion. Allegory of intra-genetic cross-breeding and opposing in-breeding as necessary for immortal survival through myth and nature.

*Nature (Space) =Time as in E(nergy)=Mass x (speed of light (time x distance)) squared; fundamental particles of energy/force and matter (Newton/Einstein/Chandra-Bose/Hubble: Universe faster expanding and over Time naturally cooling entropy/thermo-dynamics.

* Gaia/Uranus Hera/Zeus: Callisto Cassiopea Andromeda Perseus et. al. Clash of The Titans ancient Greek and Roman mythology comics franchise (Mary Carey/Dan Speigal 1980-). Opal Luna Saturnyne: Her Royal Whyness: Marvel comics (Stan Lee): SuperHeroes and Excalibur comic books. Dave Thorpe/Alan Davis Captain Britain 1982. Andromeda (Gene Roddenbury TV series 2000). Guardian and Omni-versal Majestrix SuperTeam Manga anime films and numerous video-games based on the globally shared character' characteristics and relationships of ancient and modern myth and legend.

* Gaia (Saturn-moon/Earth-Mother) daughter and wife of Uranus (The Sky God; Nature). Uranus castrated by Kronos (Time) at Gaia's command their children consumed (except for Zeus by trickery traded as a cloth wrapped rock) and exiled scattered throughout the Solar System. From Uranus' blood, as sea, air and earth, came Harpies and Furies (from Hell), or as The Kindly (or gracious) Ones, seeking vengeance for lies and false oath. (Sandman: Neil Gaiman 1996 graphic novel). The Revenge of Gaia (ecological science): James Lovelock 2000.

* Natural Justice: The unproven notion of de-ontological (non-anthropic) Universal moral imperatives (Kant) or original sin (Biblical/Marvel comics) as inescapable natural-sin and concupiscent desire, weakening of moral free-will, personal and public duty/order.

* Confucian ideal of fairness and justice in family and social relationships. Living in righteousness ideal absolute (Junzi) in contrast to Xiaoren (petty egoistic) with mutual equal respect for age and ability (sagacity).

* In religious philosophy, as Boethius and the question of absolute/relative Free Will. The Absolute is the concept of (a form of) Being which transcends limited, conditional, everyday existence. The manifestation of the Absolute has been described as the *Logos*, Word, the *Rta* or *Ratio* or Reason. Related concepts are the Source, Fountain or Well, the Centre, the Monad or One, the All or Whole, the Origin (*Arche*) or Principle or Primordial Cause,the Sacred or Holy or Utterly Other (Otto), the Form of the Good (Plato), the Mystery, Nirvana, the Ultimate, the Ground or Urground("Original Ground"). It is sometimes used as an alternate term for the more commonly used God of the Universe, the Divine or the Supreme Being ("Utmost Being"). The principle of plenitude which asserts the Universe contains all of unchanging existence including choice/free-will, all possibilities ultimately unknowable.

* Mary Shelley: Frankenstein or The Modern Prometheus 1817. A philosophical existential humanist view of technology and progress including free-will and the emotions (of sin and corruption as well as appreciation of good and beauty) and essentially non-mechanistic (existential choice). Also: The Last Man (1826).

*Male (XY chromosomes) yielding warrior conflict competition possessiveness driving (XX) fe-male mate selection for paired wholeness as healing/closure/equality moving-on through choice: a reductionist explanation of mostly male survival conflict (fight) and female consensus for survival (food). Traditional family (adult parent child in Transactional Analysis) rivalrous/jealous love triangles and the question of whether human civilisation is developing Humanist/Anthropic Universalist morality, or is determined /fixed in immorality or amorality, is answered with the optimistic explanation that indicates that societies worldwide are generally less violent and more prosperous in terms of (enough) provision for all and longer lives (exponentially, from known and extrapolated historical records; Pinker: The Better Angels of Our Nature (2010) 'from saving (religious ideological) souls to saving actual lives'; Kant: Perpetual Peace 1795. Yoko Ono – The Feminisation of Society 1971.

* Storm Ororo is a mutant superhero recruited by Professor X to the X-Men comic series Uncanny X-Men fighting with or against Magneto. Working for world peace and equality (Marvel Comics Stan Lee/Jack Kirby 1965-).

*Crossing The Line: An equatorial nautical rite of passage/line of familial social sexual acceptance, respectability and practicability between species' genetic and stellar atomic physically and chemical related (periodic table) through cosmic stellar evolution, and categorical but social-distinctions (tribalism/ethnicity/ cultural / political/religious class/ caste / language/ gender). Yet, Journey to the West (Ming Dynasty China mid-600 me account: Wu Cheng'en (author): 'Nothing in this world is difficult, but thinking makes it seem so. Where there is true will, there is always a way.'

* Thing: Existential phenoma physio-logical-being or entity in and of itself: both object and subject. Ancient Viking Norse Germanic democratic electoral house. Also called a Meet. From proto-Indo-European *ten*: to stretch time (in-diplomacy). French: cho(i)se(ir) (object and to choose: object/activity). The Thing (Marvel Comics –The Avengers, enemies including Impossible Man and Dr. Doom).

* Gog and Magog places and peoples. Ancient EurAsian Mongolian Khazar and Hun nomads. Biblical and Quranic Revelations of Apocalypse and The End of Days. Also Madoc the Great (legendary King of Albion/Welsh Giant defeating Brutus of Troy).

* Reference to Eliot The Wasteland: Life (perfumed candles) as games of skill (chess players) and chance (the 'wicked' cards) of genetic evolution.

* Heaven (sky, firmament, where gods dwell, afterlife, paradise) has many interpretations from the profane to the absurd. In Buddhist freedom from suffering in life, or nothingness: Nirvana, the candle flame blown out, the perfect solution to life is death. In mythology and most Theist religions it is freedom from a Hellish threatening Underworld or life of eternal pain. Hell may also be neutral, as Purgatory; Limbo; Darkness. Pantheist and pluralist views suggest rather a continuum to and from and of life.

* The etymology of the term happy is from Indo-European English hap (fortunate/ blessed) also linked with the pre-dynastic Egyptian God/dess Hapi (who combines both male and female) whose hieroglyph indicates union with Ra (Sun) representing the fields and animal fertility, and the flooding river (Nile) and source of life itself (with the creation figures Isis/Osiris) in plenitude. as enough (Gou) of All (Pan) Earth and Sky/waters (Tan (nit) (China/N. Africa/Greco-Roman) i.e. the sufficiency rather than necessity for life in The Universe/river (of life), and thus the requirement for ritual and worship.

* Quasar Red-Giant to White Dwarf dying ageing stars in The Solar Galactic-Halo as lit quanta around The Centre (supermassive Black-Hole/non-luminous star) of The Galaxy: The Milky Way/Ashen Sky Path (Africa. Nordic, Innuit): Chinese Dragonic Pacific Andean Aztec Great Tree Bird/ Volcanic Oceanic-Sky River of creation, and nightly re-creation.

* Sartre: Being and Nothingness (existential/phenomenological philosophical work; 1943). The Wall (play 1939). The appearance of Self and Other in the world corresponds 'to a congealed

sliding of the whole universe' (as in travelling through the birth canal) or 'a surging up of the world' as Life, and the fundamental notion that a continuous divided duality plural reality precedes single essence (the thing, or individual, in as of itself, but *for* other). A person can at a Time choose to be a good person, instead of a cruel person. We can choose to be either cruel or good, but are neither of these essentially. We can choose, either war or peace, although life itself may be a constant internal/external battling and unavoidable fact(icity) of the past, consciousness is both a limitation and a condition of continuous freedom, as the intrinsic personal value placed on obvious facts in the world, including Our Own Being, and that of Other (s) as subject/object, room/café/scene/landscape etc. The constant phenomenological Look or Gaze of Other (as God perhaps, or personal Conscience) in dreams and otherwise real shared decision-making and information sharing of action as the always constrained but real relatively free-will that we experience whilst alive (e.g. whether to kill or commit suicide, to have a reason to live (Camus: The Myth of Sisyphus 1942).

* Quarks are measurable fundamental directional up/down particles composing atomic nucleic Neutrons then Protons producing electron-neutrinos and positrons. The Quark and the Jaguar (Gell-Mann 1963); Quark, an otherwise absurd irrational paradoxical and non-mathematical word (three-quarters mustered of what? Nothing? Everything?) derived from James Joyce: Finnegan's Wake (1939):

' Three quarks (quarts) for Muster Mark!'

Words as replacement objects. The Cry of The Gull: Emmanuelle Laborit (actress; autobiography 1998): *Words have struck me as odd ever since my childhood. The simplest of concepts were even more mysterious.* Yesterday, tomorrow, today. *My mind worked in the present. What did* past *and* future *mean? I took a giant leap forward when, with the help of sign language, I understood that yesterday was behind me and tomorrow was in front of me. That was huge progress. Later, I realized that other words referred to people. Emmanuelle was me. Papa was him. Mama was her. Marie was my sister. I was Emmanuelle, an individual. I had a name, therefore I existed.*
Also see : Room: Emma Donaghue novel 2010 film: for the use of words as objects themselves.

Sartre: Les Mots (autobiography 1953)

* Orion Galactic spur arm, containing the constellation Orion the Hunter with the Centaurean Archer at the centre of The Galaxy, Universal Giant/Skull grin.

* Every/All/none/some/thing 'Ness': The existential riddle is generic (from Gotham/Batman TV series 2015).

*Nessus (anti-Hero) as naturally evil/deadly lying (tricking and reciprocated killing with a blood poisoned embrace. As Marduk and Tiamat with mutual poisoned arrows; as Romeo and Juliet, mutual murder/suicide as true love; or simply naïve, immoral. As Hercules / Hero only ever aiming for reciprocated Love and Heroic/Other status within the Universe.

* The World Hunter constellation (Greek Orion/Roman/Venus (Virgil 70-9 BME. Loved by Aurora, boasted and killed by Artemis' scorpion constellation. Recognised since ancient times, with The Great Bear (Greek Ursa; Arabic Dubhe) depicted in pre-historic cave painting, agricultural/religious rite and ritual, story, and film (Hubble satellite telescope 3D dir. Toni Myers 2010).

* The Centre of The-Galaxy: a bulging mass of ancient starmass with a hyper-massive central Black-Hole and *dancing* magnetic-field polarising light in the direction of the Sagittarian-Centaur (Archer) constellation.

*Mriga (sacred-deer constellation) (Bambi novel Felix Saltem 1923; Disney films 1942) friendly, approachable, hunted for food, killed). The Chinese/Indian star name pre-dating the Egyptian, Arabic and Greco-Roman hunter/ beast cosmologies. Named for the lunar house or mansion (China/India) of the Giant (Arabic; Greek Orion) nebulae.

* Enki African mythological immortal Earth-Mother and father Abassi (meaning stern rigid uncompromising First Cause). Sudan East Africa Enki who from the virginal sky giving birth to a male and female formed from claypot and saliva/semen/milk. Biblical Adam (Sanskrit: progenitor) and Eve (living-One/ source of life).

*Baba Yaga/Draga or Babushka is a Slavic/Russian supernatural figure, confounding crone, with pestle and mortar, sandcastling order creating less change out of infinite chance. Truth set-free. who may help or hinder through their 'babbling' advice.. Linked with Peron/Jupiter the God of creation (Mikhail Lomonozov 1755 Russian Grammar; Vladimir Propp morphological folklorist 1928) and contrasted with Vasilia The Fair (as Grimm's fable Cinderella, Baba Yaga may be three cruel sisters.

*Land and Sea evolutionary para-phyletc species including whale/hippo/pig/deer/ horse: The Aquatic Ape (theory): Elaine Morgan (1971).

* The triune-brain formed like coral; in evolutionary neuro-psychology(MacLean /Sagan/Lynne Margalis) is the primitive reptilian-mammalian limbic neo-cortex attached to the earliest forebrain in all animals.

* Loki: Norse God or Jotun/Giant and both gender and animal, trickster or enabler (Prometheus), shape-shifter. The Father of Hel (Being) who is appointed by Odin (magic wanderer as Professor X) with Freya/Frigg (prudential justice, foreknowledge, wisdom, fertility) with Ororo (gold (tears) the heavenly weaver, and wearer of the famed sun/moonstone necklace/torc) which Loki seeks to steal back from their son Justice/Boldr tricked and slain by his blind brother Hodr, bringing on Ragnorak. Hel is to reign over The Underworld, or Hell. She is half-blue/black and half-red/white (i.e. shades of brown), and rules over vast mansions (as Indo-European and Chinese star houses of the sky, the stars of the dead (ancestral history) being her servants/advisors (as original African animist and ancestor worship). Loki is father to The Dragonic World Sea Serpent Jormongadr, Ouroboros (India/Egypt) or World's End Anaconda (Aztec/Inca) tail eating serpent/dragon. Loki is also as the European Commedia del Arte of Pulcinella, or Mr Punch, the Lord of misrule, non-self-reflective and born of the Goddess of Earthly sorrow, and self-consuming wolverine Fenir, or Fire SunBird, mythic terrifying mo(o)nster and all as Carl Jung Social Archetypes of a collective unconscious, of a pre-ego dawn state of protection from fear and danger, of primal individuation in analytic psychology, and practical familial bio-social evolution.

* The analogy here of society or civilisation with the behaviour and possibly inner thoughts or language as economics in terms of The Hunt, haggling barter, feeding family; of bees and non-human species (Adam Smith The Wealth of Nations 1776; Mandeville 1705 The Grumbling Hive; Gordon Tullock 1994 The Economics of non-Human Societies (Univ. of Indiana)).

* Hu-Man. Manu (Hindu/Indo-European proto-plast/pro-genitor). -Hu is a Chinese word for an ancient vessel, a Persian Sufi and Egyptian God, a Hopi spirit being, a Welsh legendary figure. Man is an ancient Indo-European Sanskrit written word, with an earlier Asiatic spoken meaning as 'Earthly-Being'. TV series and video-game Chinese Paladin book 2010; The Myth (video-game)2015.

* Anansi (Greek Arachne) weaver: African trickster-God and spider-myth as possibly the oldest spoken story in the oral tradition: web of mind and cosmoglyph of the calabash or baobab tree(EarthCentre) of knowledge and wisdom. Stories stolen from the leopard snake and hornet; then from the top of a baobab or silkworm cotton tree held onto before let go ignoring advice to strap the pot onto the back and so to have two hands free to climb, and the pot dropped into a rainstorm, then into a stream, then river and sea, then Ocean in confusion, and for all the world to know. Kwaku-Anansi Marvel comics superhero 2012 based on SpiderMan.

* Fight Club. Existential modernist novel: Chuck Pahunuik (1996); also film David Fincher (1999); comic book David Mack Cameron Stewart 2015. Life's perceived permanent and unavoidable fight to exist/succeed/be-occupied/ not-bored; or be subjugated by Other.

* Chaos/Creation mythological reference to 'blood and pus-gatherers' (war and disease) from Aztec/Inca South and Meso-America.

* Heraclitus (in Plato: Cratylus. As quoted by one Simplicus): 'Ever-newer waters flow on those who step into the same rivers.' Democritus: 'Nothing exists except atoms and empty space; everything else is opinion.'

* Iris Murdoch philosopher/novelist: Sartre: Romantic Rationalist (1953): The Sea The Sea (1958) from Paul Valery poem and The Odyssey (Atwood/Barker et al) memoir as 'forever restarting home'. The inner philosophical problem of morality (goodness) and non-robotic free-agency with shared social ethical/moral reality, and responsibility in religious or secular faith: Humanism (How We Think: 1910: John Dewey) and Existentialism (Jean Paul Sartre (1905-1980: Philosophic and critical essays). The Platonic dilemma of what is morally good is (allegedly) commanded by God because it is morally good, or if (allegedly) commanded by God. If God exists at all, then, the question of God's own existence becomes a moral question, and open to discussion and doubt. Morality is a human, possibly scientific universal but synthetic relativistic conditional, social and political
function (democratic as against dictatorial power relationship).

* Tannit (Phoenician north Africa) or Tan-Gou (Arabic / Chinese linked to Pan Gou) an ancient fertility Goddess linked later to Hera/Junu/Astarte (Greco-Roman).

* Andean/Inca/Mayan American ancient world mythological and religious Earth-Mother and anthropomorphic creation coupling-figures.

* Chinese/Japanese Weaver Girl (Norse: Freya) and Cowherd universal creation galaxy/river myth (Nuwa and Fuxi) with children.

* The ancestral Galactic Bridge. Zhinu and Niulang: ancient Chinese Korean Japanese and Vietnamese fairy weaver-girl or spinning-damsel and mortal cowherd beseeching of disallowed love.

'Art is the expressing of One's Universal *wound* – the *wound* of living a *finite*-Life of incomplete-*meanings*...'
Neuro-scientist Raymond Tallis – quoted in Grayson Perry: Playing to the Gallery (Penguin books 2015).

* Nuwa (f) and Fuxi (m) are Chinese first mortals, and twins: as Lif and lifthrasir (Norse Love and Love of Life respectively) surviving final war Ragnorak by hiding in the Tree of Life. As Meshia and Meshiame (ancient Persia/Iran: born from a sacred tree). Egyptian goddess Isis and Osiris. (sibling parents). As biblical Adam and Eve and the garden of Eden and Tree of Knowledge goodness/evil and free-will. Biblical/Quranic love story of Yusef and Zuleika (Persian poet Jami (1414-92). Other legendary human tribal/social creation and love stories across continents, and most often as Sun and Moon.

* Sche-hera-zade: as of the storied One Thousand and One Nights (ancient original Asiatic fables); Hero/Hera; Priya (Sanskrit: beloved. Also comic book heroine Priya-Shakti) also Friya (Norse): Earth-Mother Goddess' as weavers of stories and of -the heavens.

* Babylonian Marduk (Sun God/Earth being Pan) represents assumed male sacred bullish/volcanic superiority and Tiamat (Tan-Gou) female (Moon/sacred cow/water) and potential chaos (irrational jealousy rage) ensuing from their partnership. Tiamat and Marduk are Mesopotamian and North African figures of primordial creation and civilisation deciding the fate of the living and dead.

* The End of Great-ness. Beyond the Centre of The Galaxy looking towards The Zone of Avoidance of indifference or visible exclusion area from Earth. The Great Galactic Wall.

* Zelda is a modern feminine battling computer-game character. Ganondorff-Amiibo is Giant-warrior/viral antagonist. Link is the self-styled game-player.

* Pacific-Australian mythological named originator creator coupling Eingana (Earth Mother dreamtime snake) from a waterhole at a bamboo creek. Holding everything and all life (animals birds snakes children) inside her connected by sinews that when broken life ends; and Barriaya (male spear opening the vagina for black fellows to appear with the flooding waters.

* 'The fairest most beauteous One' as judged by Zeus (Jupiter) of Hera, Athena,
and Aphrodite, who then select through Paris, to Helen of Troy, leading to the disastrous Trojan War of Godly/Regal revenge, sexual attractiveness / jealousy; as Cassiopea/Andromeda, and of familial inheritance.

* The Golden Apple: EarthCentre/beauty poisoned of Discord: as Asiatic derived European fairy tales: Prince Charming; Cinderella; Snow-White. (Brothers Grimm, Children's and Household Tales, 1812 Germany) The Royally wicked sister/step-mother and most beautiful otherwise living happily ever after (heaven).

* Pan-Dora (All-Hope) with Prometheus' (fire/industry/technology) paternal-sister by Zeus; Hesiod: Of Works and Days (750-650 before the modern era). As Anansi of all the worlds knowledge, Pandora has a secret container and knows of all the world's ills.

*Hilda's Street: Norse name for The-Galaxy/Milky Way; Asia/Americas: Heavenly Path; *Ashen* Cloud. The outer Asteroidal-Belt so-called Hildas are a significant 3-point orbital cluster stabilising the whole of the Solar-System (as the 5 Lagrange points).

* Tennessee Williams drama: Cat on a Hot Tin Roof (1955): sporting fair-play games and any belief including Humanism as faith (in humanity for the most part) against nihilism (Dostoevsky: The Idiot (1866) and Crime and Punishment (1869); Thomas Hardy: Tess (1891); Margaret Atwood: The Blind Assassin (2000). The Penelopliad (based on The Odyssey) 2005).
Buddhist feminine and masculine inter-related creation trinities, astronomy and astrology using mythological legend as history story-telling star-charts (earliest known: Sanskrit: Lagadha: Vedanga-Jyotisha India 7-600 BME).

* Cocuy is a tiny unseen bugbear click fire-beetle or Giant-dragon devilish trickster-image brought out in purification ceremonies and stories and to scare children into obedience/understanding/self-preservation (Hispanic/Portuguese/Brazilian) Lesh (Slavic/Russian) Pillan/Mohan (India/Americas); Monoke/Oni (Japan spirit of a thing or object/manga). Tricksters are global mythical harmless fun-learning characters led by The Signifying Monkey (Henry Gates 1989) based on probably the most ancient known World mythology. Anansi (American Uncle Remus/Brer Rabbit: African-American spoken-word trickster-mythological character, akin to Anansi and African Tiger: oral moralising and socially familial and personally protecting stories (parables) Joel Chandler Harris (1880 American plantation-folklorist).

Octavia E. Butler: The Patternist Series (science-fiction) atomic-cosmological genetics, transformation, morphosis,

* Game Theory (von Neumann 1944) shows a determined tendency in animals to shared survival through advantageous collaborative effort and generalised perhaps instinctive cost/benefit analysis, zero-sum, and de-limiting minimax (fairness) decision-making in daily commerce and social activity. This is also shown in chimpanzee behaviours (Jane Goodall 1986: The Chimpanzees of Gombe) intra and inter group behaviour, daily battles with occasionally individually deadly consequences, rare if ever deliberate warfare or genocide.

* P & Q are the nomenclature/tags given the top and bottom genetic stems (or arms and legs) of the centriolar or cellular genetic nuclei, double-helix coiled strands around cylindrical tubules of DeoxyriboNucleic Acid (DNA nitrogen bases (ATGC) of phosphate carbohydrate sugars with hydrogen bonds; Watson and Crick and Rosalind Franklin – London/Cambridge 1953). Barbara McClintock (1902-1992) for the discovery of genetic transposition. Rita Levi Montalcini (1909-) for embryonic stem call nerve growth factor. Anastasia Makar'eva (1974-) for Biotic regulation.

* Here a very brief textual history of recorded thought and belief in writing from the earliest Ishango bone calendar and counting sticks of the central African lakes, to the picto-ideograms of China/Japan to the Pacific Australias and the Americas, and via Indian Sanskrit to the Arabian, Ethiopian and Zimbabwean Civilisations; Sumerian carved numeric script, for accounting land and goods, and then servicing spoken language. The Afro-Asiatic, Latin and Cyrillic and Indo-European languages written printed luminous painted, and now tele-printed computer text as information technology/programming as atomic DNA/RNA genetic-energy/mass constructs of relatively stable nucleon proton and moving electron-cloud fields. Quantum field computational theory. Biological structural quantum logic processing number/words. Remote control and Wi-Fi radiated through the electron nuclear-atomic dense mass of space and from satellites in low to zero mass open-space.

Plutino's are significant asteroids between Neptune and Pluto of the Oort and Kuiper outer-asteroid belts at the edge of The Solar System. Each in conic-orbits confusing and complicating together the complex three and five point bodies/points relatively stabilising The Solar-System in order for life to evolve on Earth.

Phoebe/Ceres/Demeter (moon) Egyptian Greco-Roman Earth Mother of Freedom (Libera).

*Sedna (Innuit) mutilated and murdered by her parent's (Nature (Storm)/Time (Moment)) in jealousy and retribution for her attractive good looks and refusal to marry in dis-obedience marries a dogfish and sinking to the bottom of the Ocean, rising as a seal and becoming revered of The Arctic Hunt luring sailors and fish to their fate.

* The seven stars of Pleaides (full sailing ship) are prominently and obviously known across all world myth and cosmology rising and sinking, placed between Orion and Taurus. They are most often referred to as familial/tribal sisters (Greece/Java) or brothers (Native American Lost Boys), animals (Norse hens of Freya/China white tiger/Berber cat) at war (Indo-European (ambush/panoply armour) or peace , seed planting (Bantu) harvest (Andean) and hunting (native American) marketplace (Aztec) cooking/marriage/birth/creation (Hindu/Indigenous Australia).

*Centaurean King Father-son Prince Nessus, monster, who out of jealousy for and lying of Hera's innocent love, kills Hercules in duel with a poisoned sword, a false-rival goaded in turn killed by Heracles/Hercules the Hero embracing Nessus anti-Hero with his poison blood soaked tunic defeating such Heroic moral-Being, all in passion being without morals, especially in revenge. Revenge is best served cold – old saying.

* Reference to Native American and Ancient Chinese story-myth legend of creation and destruction.

* Knowledge/truth by presence, consciousness, selfhood, conscience, soul. Descartes: I think therefore I am. (Discourse 1637). (Avicenna 980-1037: floating/falling man thought experiment (and magic mystic trick). Duality of Reality (The Universe) and how we each see our personal universe (s) through our senses and organic additional brain (s)' The Universe, multiverses in momentary-time, positional-space (dimensions) and temperature differential as motion, being.

* Dark matter and energy are observed through gravitational-wave lensing and anomalous velocities of galactic objects indicating that there is more matter and energy in the Universe than is directly observable. As much as 97% of the total mass and energy visible as radio heat and light waves is not in the visible spectrum and is only measurable using instrumentation. Most of The Universe is dark and observable only through gravitational effects on visible matter.

* Centre: *geometry.* the middle point, as the point within a circle or sphere equally distant from all points of the circumference or surface, or the point within a regular polygon equally distant from the vertices;a point, pivot, axis, etc., around which anything rotates or revolves:the source of an influence, action, force, etc.;a point, place, person, etc., upon which interest, emotion, etc. focuses; a principal point, place, or object: a building or part of a building used as a meeting place for a particular group or having facilities for certain activities:an office or other facility providing a specific service or dealing with a particular emergency (dictionary.com)

* Glaucus (Ovid): Giant Sea Slug. Prophetic Sea-God of Poseidon and the freshwater Nymph Naiad sibling of the salty Oceonid rescuing fisherfolk and sailors, as gracefully grateful mortal to ungrateful immortal form as Harpy/Sirens luring sailors to their inevitable fate (death) as Romanian Bohemian Dracula Vampire (Bram Stoker novel 1897) Transylvanian Serbia folklore. Africa Ashanti Adze firefly. Southern Cape large taloned bird. Madagascar/Egypt/Japan Ra-Manga eating toe nails and drinking blood (as the Portuguese/Brazilian Voodoo/Cocu). Native American animist and and Chinese dragonic Thunder and Lightning (Thor/Odin Zeus/Jupiter) and other Sky Father Gods globally.

* Adenosine triphosphate is a nucleoside triphosphate used in cells as a co-enzyme referred to as the molecular unit of currency of intracellular energy transfer. ATP transports chemical energy within cells for metabolism $C_{10}H_{16}N_5O_{13}P_3$ of the building blocks of life DNA/RNA.
*Empirical Anthropic rational democratic pragmatic Humanism: *What Humanism means to me is an expansion, not a contraction, of human life, an expansion in which nature and the science of nature are made the willing servants of human good.* John Dewey On Human Nature (1953).

* Ayn Rand: The Fountainhead (1943) and Atlas Shrugged (1957). 'A code of morals accepted by choice is a code of (individual) morality as the achievement of (individual) happiness'.

* The Great Galactic Wall: as the Universal Light Horizon and of the largest and most distant cosmological objects in the known Universe, from dying Quasar star Rings, to Digital (stellar) Constructors.

* There is an allusion here to the fictions Gold Bug (Edgar Allen Poe (1924)) and R.L. Stevenson (Treasure Island (1882)) of hidden treasure as the assumed unfair greedy and violent yet rational objective of life and the attaining of solution to life's mysteries. As Don Quixote (Cervante 1615) tilts at windmills as imaginary barriers (dragons) to seeking ideal justice or reason in the world; as hidden truth as the basis of modern detective novels (Agatha Christie/Chandler etc.) and science-fiction (Mary Shelley to Octavia Butler and Iain M. Banks). Generally in seeking ultimate absolute solutions to, or acceptance of life's intrinsic questions (particularly of personal belief, or social fairness). As alternative perspective of seeking, against assumed instinct, and shared free-will, with *enough* love, peace and understanding to satisfy life's needs and cravings: Svetlana Alexievich: War's Unwomanly Face: (Belarus 1985). Toni Morisson Beloved 1987: Mother-daughter relationships and the psychological impact of slavery and sexual crime.

* As Homer's Iliad (Trojan Wars) Odyssey (Journey) Ionia 8th century before the modern era) epic journey of discovery wherein Poseidon God of The Universal-Ocean becomes the enemy of mortal landed settled humanity. Norse: Krakon. Akkorokamui (Tiawn/Korea); Moby Dick (Melville 1851); Leviathan (biblical). Simone Weil: The Iliad or Poem of Force (1939). The Sun Queen: ancient Wa (early Japanese) Himiko Island Shamen Sovereign chosen by the populace, for peace after decades of war. From 3rd Century Chinese recorded accounts: The Three Kingdoms.

* Margaret Atwood 2005 The Penelopiad after Homer's Odyysey. Oryx and Crake (2003) "Immortality' says Crake, 'is a concept. If you take 'mortality' as being, not death, but foreknowledge of it and fear of it, then 'immortality' is the absence of such fear. Babies are immortal. Edit out the fear, and you'll be...'

* Deus Ex Machina: God of The Machine: Greek Tragedy/Mystery: plot device with divine resolving usually happy comedic ending. War of The Worlds. Tolkein's Lord of The Rings. Shakespeare: As You Like It and many others are later examples.

* Cao Xuequin: Dream of The Red Chamber/The Story of Stone (China generational novel mid 18th C) 'Dualist continuum, plurality. Truth becomes fiction when the fiction is true; Real becomes not-real where the unreal is real.' The impossibility of pure distinctions between qualities/ideals such as truth/falsity reality/unreality or natural/unnatural (can anything apart from deliberate human actions be unnatural?).

* Commonwealth (Pepys Diary 1667): 'Better things were done, and better managed under a Commonwealth than under a King.'

Termagant: English via Old French Italian three wandering as The Moon between Heaven, Earth an Hell named as Selene, Artemis and Persephone (daughter of Zeus and Demeter, Kore, Goddess of The UnderWorld); of Zoroastrian-Magician (three-handed). Norse Loki; German TiW; Celtic Tyr; Mighty God of Law and War: The Song of Roland (historical 778); Mohammed/Jesus with Apollo or Lucifer. King priests or warriors or bureaucrat. Referenced in Confucious, Chaucer, Shakespeare, Washington Irving's Rip Van Winkle short story and the video micro-game: ChiTin 1. The Machine Stops: E.M. Forster: The Eternal Moment and Other Stories (1928).

[*] Minotaur (Greek) Bull or Ox-head (Chinese) mythological guardian of The UnderWorld (as Osiris/Orion, son of Poseidon and King Minos (Crete).

[*] Due to their combined gravitational attraction and mass, it is predicted that the three largest galaxies to EarthCentre: The Local Group of The-Galaxy (The Milky/Ashen Way), with Andromeda and Triangulum will eventually collapse into each other and the Hyper-massive Black-Holes at their centres merge, or spin-off to reform creating massive gravitational waves throughout another new Universe. This Universe as a possibly Mega-massive originating three to four-dimensional directional, inward as outwardly expanding quadri-polar Universal Black-Hole, or non-luminous star.

* The-Universe itself i.e. as a single Universal Black-Hole, possibly radiating or circulating neutrinos and smaller particles as yet to be discovered (Hawking radiation) in and into *nothingness as ever reducing* atomic particle stellar galactic molecular multi-dimensional gravitational bound inspiral orbits string signal ramping wavelength-frequencies mergent then the ringing down terminably as new event horizons. With as many primordial black-holes attached or detached as there are atoms, as galactic stars and planets and moons, asteroids and comets, gas and dust clouds; and as Each of Ourselves, inside our own owned existentially integral and otherwise combining continually re-discovering truths as the here and now. Our shared worlds, as The-Universe: *This*-Universe (ref. Stephen Hawking 2009 (The Galactic-Halo; Black-Hole Starship): Marcus Chown: New Scientist 2009. Hawking 3-D map of the Universe 2016 in production at the Super-Computing Centre, Cambridge, England; as current-theory tested against immediate and recorded experiment and observation...

The Universe may or may not be cyclical continuous and long-lasting, as may humanity be so, but very likely less so. As current fact-laden science shows through the laws of thermo-dynamics, entropy and decay, and evolution, particle parity and species violation, veers from heat to cold, light to dark. The question remains as to Hu-manities' special place, or plan in *this* Universe. Since we are here and now, proof of the existence of this sometimes seemingly random free but otherwise non-random fated rushing and relinquishing of the seemingly purposeful accidental impossible. We are uniquely intelligent technological reproducing life in the Universe. Through each seed brain, whether in a Big Bang or string membrane-like creeping crawls an *almost* perfect homogenous Universal-Space of mainly and increasingly Dark Matter and Dark Energy: of light and heat waning and soon enough a Universe of immaterial energy cycling inward and outward as eventually again...*nothingness*? Or another Universe re-born and dying-again...collapsing stars and galaxy. The Galaxy, Andromeda and Triangulem from whence we most likely arrived and will return through gravitational electro-magnetic nucleation wormhole black holes bouncing back continuously, at the centre of all things, and these Universal Verses...

M.Stow. London, England, 2019.

EarthCentre: The End of The Universe: M.Stow.
ISBN-13: 978-1491017357   ISBN-10: 149101735X

Acknowledgments and permissions requested:

Paul Williams (cover and interior painting).

Emmanuelle Laborit (The Cry of The Gull 1998)

Emma Donaghue (The Room 2010)

All Ilustrations

Equatorial-Polar EarthCentre (above); below: Jupiter (with EarthCentre superimposed) and Saturn as gas-Giants failed Stars with Earth-like largest Jovian moons, and orbiting planetary dust.

EarthCentre and The Galaxy.

Andromeda-Galaxy NASA/ESA University of Washington.

Triangulum Galaxy: constellation-guide.com

ISBN-13: 978-1492746775

ISBN-10: 1492746770

The End of The Universe: Universal Verses One: Stellation

Universal Verses1: in three-parts: Stellation

1. Stellation...

2. The Universal-Axial.

3. Universal-Axial Stellation.

1. At first there was neither being nor non-being.
There was not air nor yet sky beyond.
What was its wrapping? Where? In whose protection?
Was water there, unfathomable and deep?

2. There was no death then, nor yet deathlessness;
of night or day there was not any sign.
The One breathed without breath, by its own impulse.
Other than that was nothing else at all.

3. Darkness was there, all wrapped around in darkness,
And all was water indiscriminate: then
That which was hidden by the Void, that One emerging,
Stirring, through power of Ardor, came to be.

4. In the beginning Love arose,
Which was the primal germ cell of the mind.
The Seers, searching in their hearts with wisdom,
Discovered the connection of Beings with Nonbeing.

Rig Veda (around 1400 BCE India) X, HYMN CXXIX. Creation.

The End of the Universe: Universal Verses1: Stellation: in three-parts:

1. Stellation

2. Universal Axial:

3. Universal Axial: Stellation.

1. Stellation: in three-parts:

     -Welcome to The-Universe…

     -The End of The Universe:

Between nothing and the start of everything else: without so much of a Big
Bang!

Or, as a *sumping* deep dull thumping *Thud*! Unseen unheard

But then felt enough to know that something tremendous had occurred.

By the smallest scalar sizing by any minimal metric measure

By which anything can be measured or known.

Something *incredibly* wonderful: a point of inflection pierced held

Profoundly weighty waited credible instantaneous false-vacuum framing

Zero-arrowing doubling negating neutral-booming force-field vector

Tipping tripped synergy wave-forming foaming:

-The Universe!

Transcendental! Continuous inconclusive radial half-spin up and half-spin down...

Full spin circumferential-spheroidal in magnitude-unresolving...

Indeterminate-*terminal* Being: A point in-and-of *seemingly...unendingly...*

Approaching-retreating *perfecting*-infinitude with no net-charge as yet

Assuming tentative-tenuous potential seeking-*halogenic* as if forever-becoming...

-Dia-metric *almost* equal radii-rationing:

-Dia-magnetic *neutral*-repulsion...

-Doubling negating false-*vacuum*...

-Electronic-attracting nucleating gravitational...

-Macro-Wave...

-Microwave length and frequencies...

Of every probability possible squared-area hyper-cuboid *voiding*

Hollow-surfacing One to two to three to four dimensional:

-Quadripolar...

Stretching stretched-equilateral angular-extended:

-H*exing enchanting* imaginary...

Almost Solid-block perfectly stationary-spheroidal as yet assumed:

-*S*ingularities'…

-Rotating!

-Universal!

-Stretching! Each of Us! Now! *differentially* constantly energetic-masses' *equatorial*-bulging polar-capped axial irregular-size and shape-shifting dependent on energy-mass and rate of rotation predicting-model existing:

-Universal *dense* Black-Hole…

-Macro-wave Cosmic *background*…

-Neutron-Star *core micro-wave*…foreground pulsing-Quasar-Stars and Galaxies and Atoms free-falling:

-The Universal-Space:

-The Universe!

Forming ejecting material along polar-aligned radiation-axis compressed glowing Event Horizons *lit*…

Hovering on the *shadow*-edge radiation falling-out floating collided-disorder:

-Dis-Order!

-What-Order!

-Algorythmic…

-From *purely*-lawful equational-*constant*: Functional Order…

-Now!

More than all combined entropy

Rotating-particles from shortlived virtual anti-neutral.

Double-negative annihilating reducing:

-Event Horizon…

-Proton…positron…

Lifting lilting tilting from and to

White hot *Light! Flashed!*:

       -From Absolute-Zero…

       -Points of no-return…

Nothingness-seemingly: Cold-exploded moving:

       -Linear *inflationary*-expansion expression…

       -Massively-heating from the interior…

       -Where?

       -Everywhere!

The gaps in-between evaporate freezing radiating fractional-degrees

Above:
       -Primordial Black-Hole…

       -Neutron-*blank*…

In and around: immediately suddenly from: *Nowhere:*

       -Alpha-Beta-Gamma to X-Ray…

       -Burst! Black! White! Light! Everywhere!

Bounced-back then slowed almost ceased…as instantly blown-apart again:

       -Neutron negative-electron colliding anti-electron positron…

       -As Proton Lone-Stars and together…

       -Galaxies *forming*…

Neutrino-phonon and photon forcefield

Laser-smooth uniform-equivalence *shattered clouding:*

   -Evaporate…

   -Condensate…

Collapsing crunching cool-clumping:

   -From Zero to atomic-*molecular…*

   -Compounding:

   -From Absolute Zero-Mass…

   -To potentially infinitely…

   -Finite hot-light and starry-Galaxies spinning-off…

   -*We…*

   -*Dark*-nucleons holding-off…

   -As All Dark-Energy expelled…

   -All Mass now impelling compelling Matter…

   -As Neutron-Proton Atomic-Molecular…

   -Solar-Stars…*positronic*-Planets and electronic-*Moons…*

   -Asteroid and cometary…

   -Meteoric Force-Field! Each of Us!

   -Combining-*colluding…*

   -At half the heat to light electro-magnetic energetic-speeds…

   -Each necessarily different as distant and different Place and Space
and Time…

   -Momentum…

   -Inward particle dense-region *emptying*-outward…

   -Inward collapsing again barring spiral-Galaxies…

-Spinning-off irregular ratio-mass to energetic boson-nucleic…

-Constant-steadying factors amongst the seeming chaos…

-Lone-Stars and Free-Radicals!

-Rough-shod asteroid and rounded proto-Planetary and lunar pieces…

Stilled barely moving if at all impossible yet to tell.

The *vast*-distances now *lit* by Our-Selves

Stabilising collapsing as in homogenous irregular-particle:

-Summing as-over-*history*…

-Motion-phase transition *vacuum*-bubbles

-*Imaginary*-numerals as infinite potential-Time…

-Started within our Own finite-edges…

-No boundary-beyond…

-No forward or back symmetry as asymmetrical moving…

-Arrows of Time and Nature. Nature as Time. Time as Nature.

-Each of Us: Being. The Originating *inverse square root unifying-Unit.*

Outer-tangent doubling raddi-quartering diameter

To circumference area…

Natural-logarythmic aerial-aery virtually eventually circling curved around…*almost* returning to The Start. The Beginning: Each *uniquely*-constant half-life permanent moment. Varying-finitude sprung-doubling radial-diametric distance-sprung Open-strings plucked closing-looping Almost precise repetition played Immediately drawn:

    -Naked-Neutron anti-*Quark negatively-twinned electronic magnet-*
field…

      -Proton-positive surviving…

      -A Quantum Quark for Each of Us.

      -A Quark for Each of Us.

2.

From-*Nothingness*

Dark-Beginnings perhaps *another space and timely*

Universe just like-our own:

      -White-*light*-Starship radiant…

      -Black-gapped…

      -*Wrecking*-ball breaking-up as putting-together…

      -Our-Selves! Neutral-neural blank-slate…

      -Doubly negating neutral-*nothingness*

      -Radiating-raised with no net-charge as-yet…

Assuming tentative-*tenuous* halogenic-tended:

      -Proton-positronic!

      -Outer Electron-negative *switching*-positronic *cloud*-forming force-
field *neutrino flying-off…*

      -Anti-quark paired in defence…

      -Or attack now no-longer *infinite* but finite…

      -Massive-*Nothingness…*

Stretching Universal-Space

      -Equilateral tri-angular extending…

Almost-equilateral Each of Us emanate continuously recurrent-repetitive…

Labouring working the-point:

      -Originating inverse root-squared unifying-Unit…

Each *continuously:*

-Recurrent of the originating inverse root-squared...

-Outer-tangent *diameter-to-circumference* area...

-Quadruple tri-line body-base cubed pentatonic...

Encircling:

-*Neutron-Proton Nucleon...neutrino displaying...*

Distance-surfacing balling uniquely ubiquitously

Perennially electron-sprung

Ingredient: armed and legged barring spiral-Star Galactic.

Diaphragm and girdle-bone as bafflingly-erected head and shoulders

Arms and legs as hands and feet formless-knowability *in itself* seemingly

Divine-energy...immateriel-*stomaching...*

Ourselves yet dark-hearted eaten or not To Be eaten.

Given taken as in the taking

As if by theft or trapped in-reciprocal kindness.

Traipsing-out:

-Particle microwave...

-*Wave*-Detectors...

-Detractors...

Not-so-*mysterious...*

-Hydrogenic...

-Each of Us as in Our Own Known Space and Time.

Free-travelling de-localizing...collectively a Universal WarZone.

Marching in number holding-out against

And as unto un-known unknowable-*Battle of judgment and justification...*

Continued...

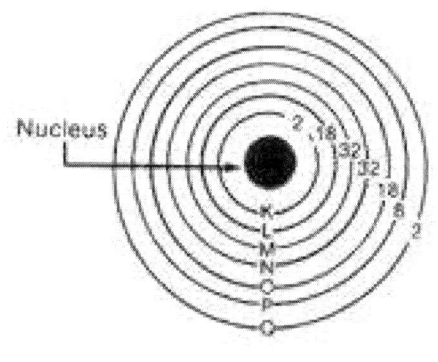

major energy level	K	L	M	N	O	P	Q
maximum number of electrons	2	8	18	32	32	18	2

Atomic nucleus and electro-magnetic cloud ring's optimum electron points of oscillation to absolute atomic number (here synthetic 112 Copernicium) The highest naturally occurring element is Uranium (92). Below: a copper atom (29) with super-conducting (in a vacuum) weakest outer-valence electron allowing field-current to pass through cable or points (aluminium silver and gold are also conductive single valance atoms).

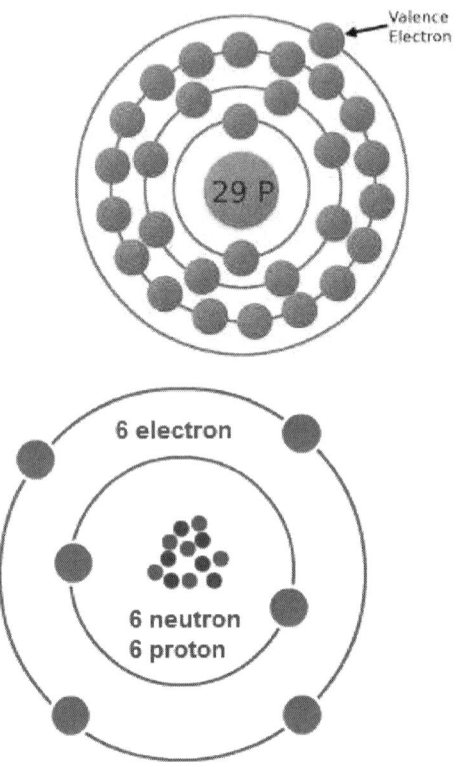

Carbon atom (above) showing stable combined neutron and proton nucleus and an equal number of stable electrons in their rings or circuits forming an electro-magnetic protective cloud or field that surrounds the nucleus at the atomic-level (as crust and mantle is heated by the Earth's molten iron nucleus/core; as Planets and Moons surround The Sun; and Stars and Galaxies surround The Galactic Centre).

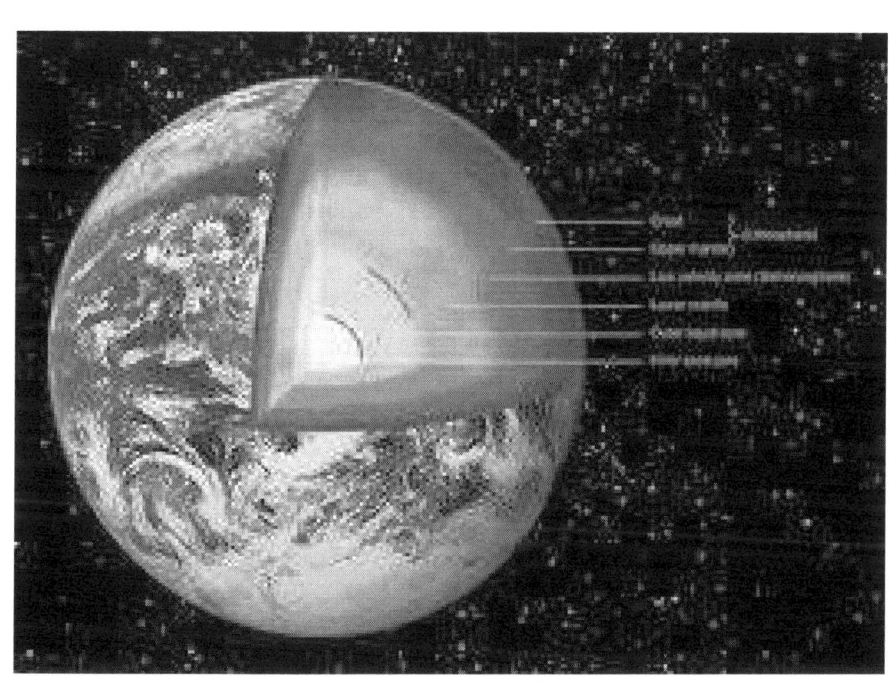

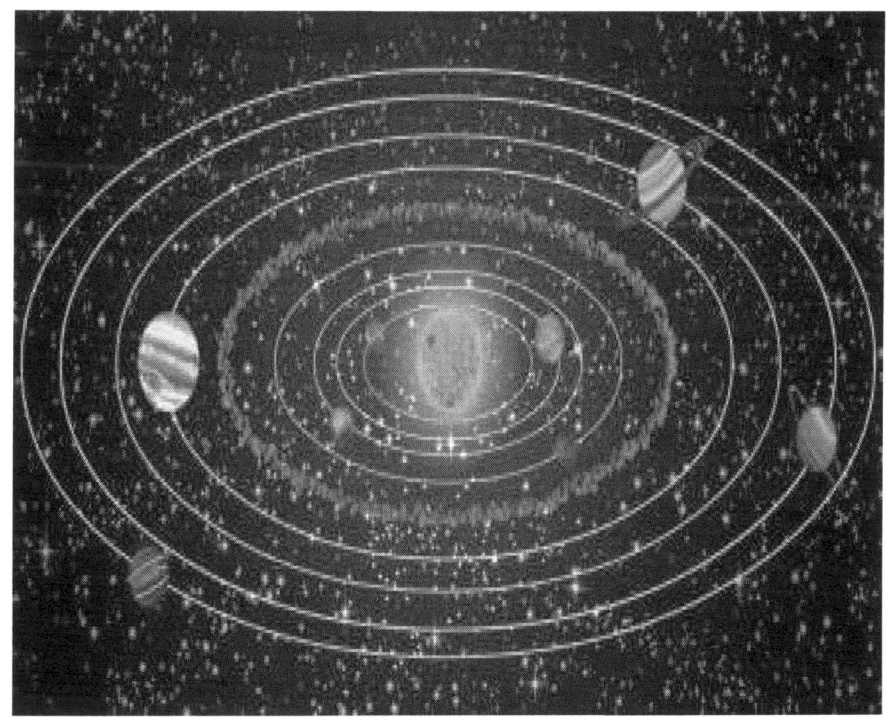

Sun

Stars in the local solar neighborhood move randomly relative to one another...

230-million-year orbit

27,000 light-years

...while the galaxy's rotation carries them around the galactic center at even higher speed.

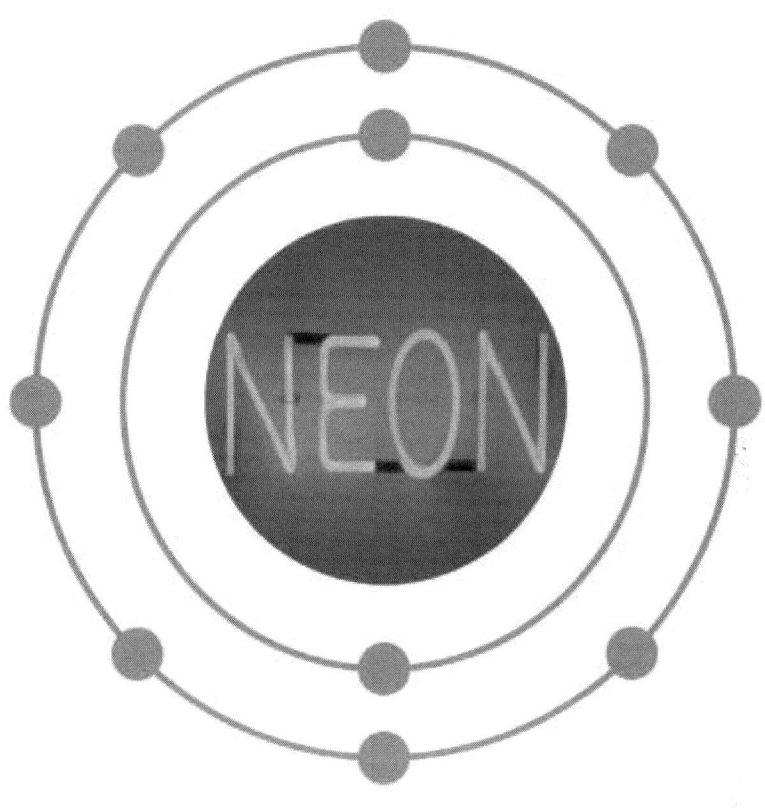

(diagrams permissions requested: chemistry.tutorcircle.com

learn.sparkfun.com thinglink.com et al)

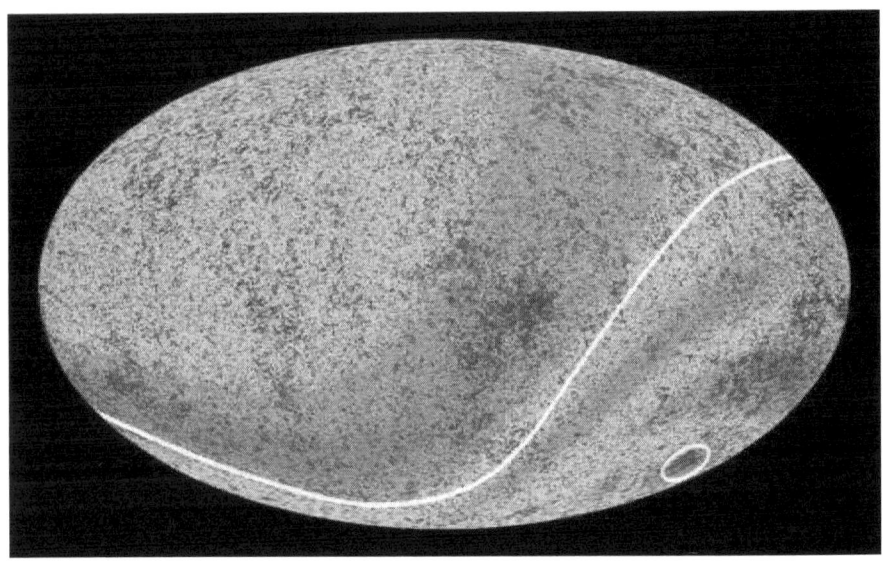

Universal Cosmic Microwave Background heat map
(European Space Agency Planck Observatory) showing the
screwed axis of quasar stellar galaxies and orientation as hot
and cold patches spread evenly to unevenly around the axis
and edges, and in the direction of a large void, in the lower
right corner. The overall shape is determined from the
perspective of The Earth/Space telescopic field of light, as an
expanded ellipse from within, with Earth as the unseen centre,
and beyond which is unknown. The Cold Spot indicates a
preferred direction of travel, variation, or Dark Flow. The
galaxies are in non-random concentric circles or orbits, which
may form an overall ellipsoid quadric surface (from inside)
and enclose numerous other dimensions as nucleate string

orbitals, not unlike the actions of atoms, planets, lunar-planetary solar systems, supernovae, meteorological storm cells; or organic ovarian seed and bifurcating genetic axial nuclei; haploid diploid-zygotic gravity electronic-magnetic evolutionary nucleic-cells; Universal Cell.

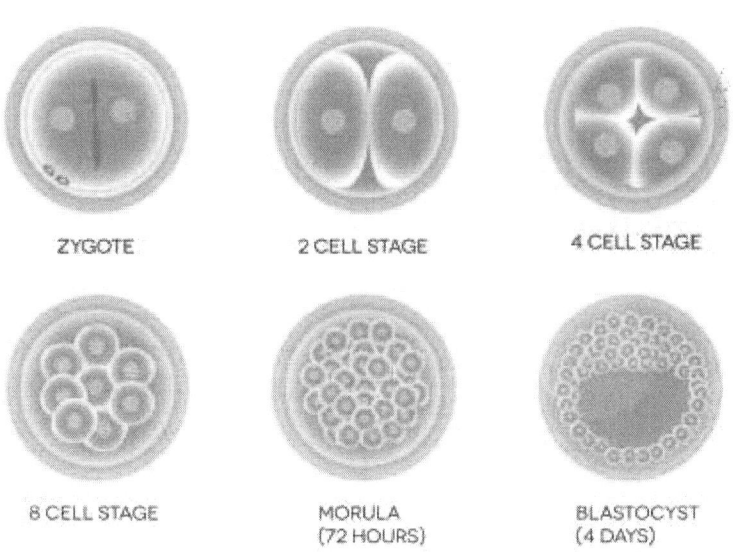

Human embryo cell growth and expansion.

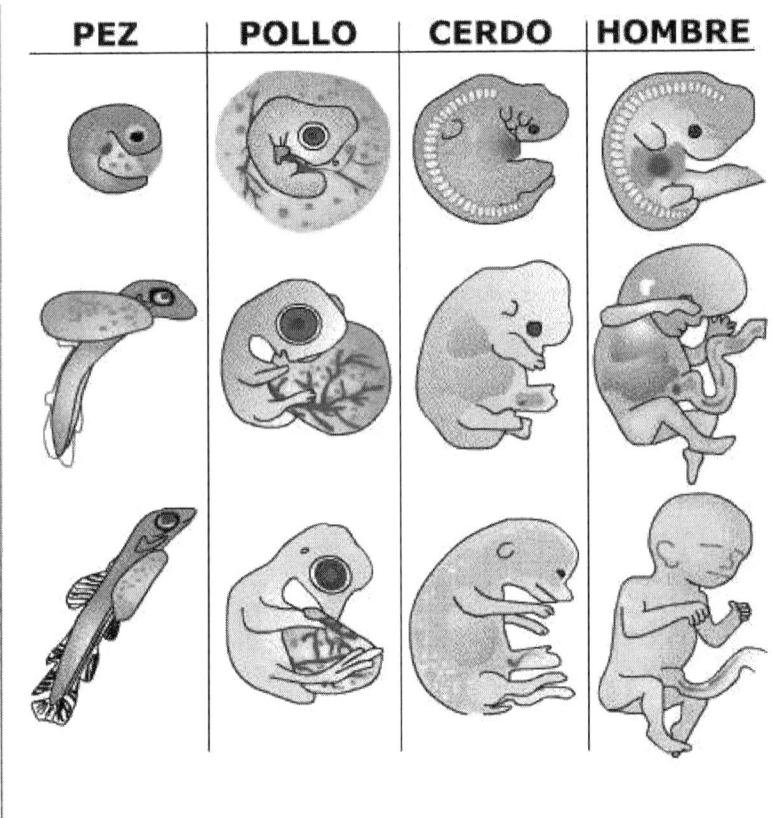

Fish, chicken, pig and human embryo development.

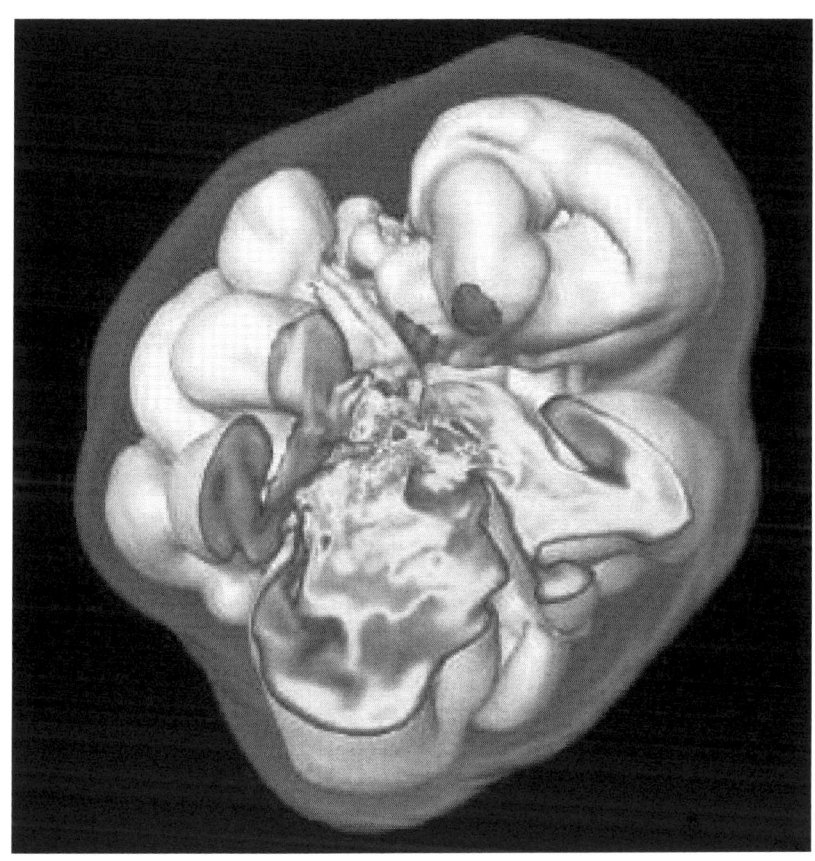

Supernova computer model (Max Planck Institute)

Osiris/Isis sibling progenitors of Earthly Humanity (with Earth (Geb) and Sky (Nut)).

A Science fiction-faction production.

Invention, it must be humbly admitted, does not consist in creating out of void but out of chaos.

Of what strange nature is knowledge! It clings to a mind when it has once seized on it like a lichen to a rock.

My dreams were all my own; I accounted for them to nobody; they were my refuge when annoyed - my dearest pleasure when free.

Mary (Woolstencraft/Godwin) Shelley: Frankenstein, or The Modern Prometheus (original novel 1818); and The Immortal Mortal (short story 1833).

New edition with Creative Commons photo-illustration all

This Photo by Unknown Author is licensed under CC BY-SA

(except and including where shown on the print)
plot summary references and text notes critically updated.

7/2/2020 M.Stow London, England.

M.Stow12

ISBN-13: 978-1491017357

ISBN-10: 149101735X
ISBN: 9781723788413
M.Stow12 2020

Printed in Great Britain
by Amazon

53264231R00143